A STRAIGHTFORWARD GUIDE TO TAKING YOUR OWN LEGAL ACTION

Foreword by Lord Woolf, Master of the Rolls.

By Laurence Kingsley

"The place of justice is a hallowed place"
From "Of Judicature" by Francis Bacon 1561-1626

Illustrations by Jake Baum
Straightforward Publishing

I

Straightforward Publishing Limited
38 Cromwell Road, Walthamstow
London E17 9JN.

British Library Cataloguing in publication data. A catalogue record for this book is available from the British Library.

ISBN 1899924 36 1

Printed by BPC Wheaton Ltd, Exeter
Cover photograph by Laurence Kingsley
Cover design by Straightforward Graphics

FOREWORD

It is now clear that more and more litigants are going to decide to conduct their own litigation. Usually the reason is that there is no alternative. Legal Aid is not available and the costs are beyond the litigant's means.

However conducting litigation when you are not a lawyer is by no means straightforward. Formal procedures have to be complied with. Although the reasons for some of the rules may not be obvious, they all exist because experience over the years has shown them to be necessary. They are however now very complex indeed and prove to be a formidable obstacle in the way of a litigant who wants to bring proceedings.

The Small Claims Court is designed to enable litigants in person to bring or defend their own claims for sums up to £3,000. However, outside the Small Claims Court, the position for non-lawyers conducting litigation is very different . I have made recommendations in my report on Access to Justice which is now being implemented which I hope will improve the position. New simpler and more intelligible core rules were published together with my report. When those new rules come into existence they should improve the position.

However litigants who are acting for themselves will still need assistance even when the new rules are in force. Until they are in force their need is even greater. This is where this book has an extremely useful role to play. In less than 150 pages it manages to meet its aims of providing a straightforward guide. It is written in clear and readily understandable language and provides the basic knowledge which the lay litigant needs. I am sure that the non-lawyer for whom this book is intended, will find it of great value. Even an experienced litigator will find it a handy ready reference book. Its importance however is that it will help the non-lawyer to conduct litigation without expensive assistance. In this way it will improve access to justice. It is because it will do this that I warmly commend this book and congratulate Laurence Kingsley.

Lord Woolf   *25 March 1997*

ACKNOWLEDGMENTS

My object in writing this book has been to try to provide a guide through the minefield of civil procedure and to indicate and simplify the main rules likely to affect the litigant in person. For many years I have believed that the Rules of the Supreme Court and the County Court Rules should be merged and simplified. I have been considerably encouraged in this project by the work and resulting proposals of Lord Woolf and his committee, who have produced "Access to Justice".

I thank Lord Woolf for his kind and generous foreword and Jake Baum for his witty illustrations.

I would also like to thank for their encouragement those litigants in person, to whom I have given assistance, in particular Jane Broughton and Celine La Freniere.

I am indebted for their advice and revisions to the Senior Master of the Queens Bench Division, Robert Turner, Master Miller, Master Murray and Taxing Master Seager Berry for their help and revisions on sections dealing with applications, injunctions and summary judgment, evidence and costs respectively.

I am grateful to the publishers of Bullen & Leake and Jacob's Precedents of Pleadings Thirteenth Edition for permission to reproduce two of their precedents.

Finally, I would like to thank Jane Young for her patience and careful typing and my publisher Roger Sproston for his guidance.

Laurence Kingsley   *January 1997*

TAKING YOUR OWN LEGAL ACTION

Foreword by Lord Woolf-Master of the Rolls.

You the Plaintiff in the County Court 113

You the Defendant in the County Court 141

INTRODUCTION

Some Common Misconceptions and some Home Truths

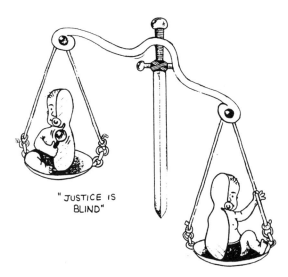

"JUSTICE IS BLIND"

It is said that **justice is blind**, which means that the law is not concerned with personalities or whether litigants be powerful or weak, good or bad or black or white. It is certainly **not deaf** and will listen to any reasonable claim; sometimes it is **not silent** and will indicate whether or not a person has a good case.

"Justice is truth in action", said Benjamin Disraeli (1804-1881) in the House of Commons on 11 February 1851. Our justice, however, is not concerned with **the truth** but only interested in deciding between competing sets of facts. This is because our legal system is not **inquisitorial** but **adversarial**.

Nor are our courts particularly eager to expound general principles of liability in favour of anyone, who appears to be hard done by: there is a particular concept known as *damnum sine iniuria*, which in plain English means that there can be **loss without legal injury.** This occurs where one suffers an injustice without there being any legal remedy. For example, a person could have an accident and suffer very

Taking your own Legal Action

"ADVERSARIAL"

substantial injuries but be unable to obtain compensation because he cannot prove that his injury was caused by the deliberate or negligent act of any legal person ie an individual or company. This situation has obviously occurred on countless occasions and there have been many judicial pronouncements, deploring the absence of "no fault compensation" in our law. The courts, however, will often seek to develop or expand the existing remedies. Law is a bottomless pit" - John Arbuthnot (1667-1735).

Consequently to win your case you have to find the right pigeon-hole ie your set of facts must be similar to, if not identical with, a previous case, where it was **declared** that there was such a right known to the law. This is called a **precedent**; the precedent system is one of the principal differences between the Law of England and Wales and the law in most foreign jurisdictions, where they tend to apply general principles to individual situations. The precedent systems works from the particular to the general, whereas other (foreign) systems of law work from the general to the particular. To put it another way, general principles of law are only laid down when a sufficient body of individual cases or precedents has come into existence.

Lawyers follow in the wake of the body of law as surely as day follows night! Lawyers of course have rarely been popular - but probably for the wrong reasons. Generally speaking they are neither dishonest nor exorbitant in their charges; they are often conscientious, competent and even charitable. The real problem is that they tend to conspire - often unconciously - to maintain the mystique of law, keeping their clients in the dark or failing to explain the law and procedure. A good lawyer is one, who not only tells the client what he will do for him and what he expects the client to do to help his own case but one who also provides reasons and explanations in plain and simple English.

Another problem is one of **credibility**. However experienced he may be in assessing character, a judge can often disbelieve a truthful person and be taken in by a liar. Juries too may not be infallible. It may be a matter of interest that Mr Michael Plumbe, the Chairman of the Queen's English Society, has written: "According to the Basic Skills Agency the number of "functionally illiterate" adults in the population is "probably higher than one in six". So in any normal jury there are likely to be at least two members with literacy difficulties."

" CREDIBILITY"

Thus one already has several uncertainties or unknown factors in the equation of litigation!

But surely - you ask - isn't a **good lawyer** bound to know the likely outcome almost to the point of certainty? I regret that the answer is probably "It ain't necessarily so"! It is a myth that solicitors and barristers know the law. Although they will have studied the law for at least three years and may even have been in practice for several years, they do not know the law. Nor could they. No-one knows it all because there is far too much of it. What, however, a good lawyer should have is a basic knowledge of the area of law, in which he practises and the relevant procedure. Even a legal textbook writer does not know all the law, especially if he has merely edited the latest edition as opposed to having written the original. A good lawyer may even have some experience in or flair for advocacy or presentation. The essential qualities of a good lawyer (apart from knowledge of the basics) are the ability to know **where to find the law** and a feeling for the spirit of the law: you yourself may have been born with this flair or feel for the law. For most mortals it is, however, acquired.

Moreover, it is not just lawyers, who may not know the law. It applies also to judges. A word about **judges**: the top judges are appointed from the cream of the legal profession but there has been many a case decided by three judges where six other equally respected judges are "wrong". This can occur where the first judge decides in favour of the Plaintiff, the three judges, who sit in the Court of Appeal, dismiss the Defendant's appeal only for the five House of Lords judges to allow the Defendant's appeal by a majority of 3:2! Thus three judges can overrule six judges.

Then there is, of course, the inequality of opportunity aspect. It was once said by a judge "Justice - like the Ritz Hotel - is open to all". In fact, according to the Office for National Statistics, in the financial year ending 5 April 1995 out of some 23 million families only 49% were financially eligible for **legal aid** and over 50% of them would have to make contributions to their own legal costs. The availability of legal aid has been doing a "disappearing act" since its introduction; the present Government is intending both to squeeze the eligibility and cap the amount to be expended on legal aid. At the other end of the scale only a few people have a net disposable income of, say £60,000, which would enable them to risk losing £10,000, the likely costs of a comparatively small case.

I would imagine that you do not fall into either group and are considering becoming a **litigant in person.** Alternatively, you may simply be disenchanted with the legal profession.

Let me now dispel another myth. If you are an individual or partner (as opposed to a limited liability company) you do **not have to instruct a solicitor**: there is nothing that a solicitor can do for you that you are not entitled to do for yourself.

You may, of course, wish to enjoy the best of both worlds by acting for yourself with or without the advice of one of the far less expensive but growing band of independent legal advisers, whose fees are usually far more reasonable. This book is designed to assist the **litigant in person**. If you do choose to retain a legal adviser find out his qualifications and experience and, if satisfied, decide if you would be happy for him to work for you. But always remember: "It is not what a lawyer tells me I **may** do; but what humanity, reason and justice tell me I ought to do": Edmund Burke (1728-1797).

Before finally making up your mind, you will want to consider the advantages and disadvantages of acting in person.

The advantages:

First, nobody can ever really know your own case better than you yourself.

Secondly, although court staff and judges cannot officially "advise" you, you are likely to receive much help from the court staff - especially in the High Court - and both sympathy and latitude from the judge, who eventually hears your case, if it be not successfully settled before the trial.

Thirdly, in the High Court (but not the County Courts) there is a Practice Master, whose sole function is to advise litigants in person

Taking your own Legal Action

(and even solicitors and barristers) on practice and procedure. No appointment is necessary; it's on a first come, first served, basis.

The disadvantages:

You lack knowledge of the law and procedure and you lack experience of presentation.

This book is designed to overcome these two disadvantages by providing you with clear practical advice.

Before you start apart from your time and application, you may need **access** to Halsbury's Laws of England (Fourth Edition) for the law, Bullen & Leake and Jacob or Atkin's Court Forms (Second Edition) for your pleadings, the Supreme Court Practice or Annual Practice ("The White Book") and the County Court Practice ("The Green Book") for procedure and you may possibly wish to buy a simple textbook on the particular area of law, relating to your claim: all these books may be found in public libraries with a law section or in the Supreme Court library (in the Royal Court of Justice), which is open to the public. This is not as daunting as it sounds, as you will only be concerned with small parts of these works and only from time to time. You will also need access to a photocopier and have to have a small amount of money for court fees: see under "Fees".

Warning: This book does not purport to teach you the law nor does it claim comprehensively to summarise all aspects of procedure - the Annual Practice alone presently runs to some 4,001 pages - but it will put you on the right track!

This book only deals with claims brought or arising under the law of contract and the law of torts; it does not deal with crime, conveyancing, family law, judicial review or wills and probate.

PART 1- THE CLAIM

This book is concerned only with civil claims in contract and tort. You probably know what a contract is: basically it is a legally recognised agreement between two or more parties, in which each party is under an obligation to one or more of the other parties eg A may agree to sell B his motor car in consideration of B paying him £5,000, or C agrees to provide his services to D, who will be his employer, or E lends money to F, who agrees to repay it to E on demand or at a certain time.

Torts are more varied but some common examples are negligence, trespass to land, trespass to the person (ie assault or battery) and defamation. Some wrongs like fraud and assault, are both civil and criminal but this book is only concerned with the civil side.

a: Recognising your claim or cause of action

This may or may not be obvious. If you wish to sue your builder or the person from whom you bought you car, this will be because he has broken his **contract**. Where the contract was "silent", ie did not contemplate what was going to happen in the particular circumstances, you may need to gather some knowledge of **Building Contracts Law** or a little extra law under the **Sale of Goods Act** respectively.

Say you were injured in a motor accident, your claim would be for the tort of **negligence** so as to enable you to obtain damages for **personal injury**: see Form 1. Sometimes you can sue in contract and/or in tort eg if your solicitor was **careless** - this is not the same as not correctly predicting the outcome of a case - you will be able to claim that he failed to do the work with the skill implied by his qualifications or forgot to start your action on time. This is often called **professional negligence**. A lot of cases are brought under this head against such people as accountants, architects, doctors, dentists, lawyers, surveyors and other types of professional, to whom you will have delegated certain tasks or on whose expertise you relied. Yet again, you may have employed someone to act as your agent: see Forms 2A and B.

b: Ascertaining your cause of action

Assuming you do not already know your **cause of action**, ie the nature of your claim or its name in law, simply look through the index to Bullen & Leake and Jacob or the contents volume for Atkins until you find the subject heading, which will immediately give you a clue. Certain words speak for themselves, eg nuisance, agency, passing off, copyright, occupier's liability etc.

When you have ascertained the necessary facts for your pleading and thus your cause of action, you may wish to "read all about it" in Halsbury or some specific textbook that takes your fancy. You will probably find that textbooks vary on your chosen topic from 150 pages to 500 or 600 pages. Halsbury usually has all you need but you may find that you particularly like the style, layout and degree of detail of certain textbooks. Remember most text-books are not written for the layman, but either for the student or for the professional practitioner.

c: Limitation of Action

Most claims must be brought, ie started by the issue of proceedings, within six years of the occurrence of the event, giving you the right to sue, but a claim for damages for **personal injuries** - probably the largest single area of litigation - must be brought within three years.

There are, however, certain exceptional claims for which different time limits apply and the limitation period is usually extended for the benefit of **minors, persons under a disability,** or where the cause of action was not known to exist by the victim or concealed from him by **fraud** or other circumstances. For a detailed approach look at the Limitation Act 1980: see Volume 2 of the Supreme Court Practice.

d: Drafting your Claim

When you have gained the necessary knowledge of the relevant area of law and glanced at a few forms of precedent in Bullen & Leake and Jacob or Atkins you should set about drafting your own claim. This will be called "Statement of Claim", if it is in the High Court, or "Particulars of Claim", if it is in the County Court and is the first "pleading".

You may be able to use an existing precedent or a combination of two or more existing precedents with very little adaptation.

Even if you hope or expect to settle your claim without suing, this exercise is invaluable because it will focus your mind considerably and help you write your **letter before action** (see g. below).

Remember the **cardinal rules of pleading**.

(1)   The purpose is to inform the Defendant of your cause of action in sufficient detail to enable him to admit your claim or defend it. He is entitled not to be taken by surprise.

(2)   Ensure that your pleading contains only the essential ingredients of your cause of action, ie what it is necessary to prove to win - no more and no less. If it lacks an essential ingredient, you will fail! If it has unnecessary ingredients, you will have added to your task the unnecessary burden of proving these facts.

(3)   Set out the essential facts but **not the evidence**, by which you hope to prove them. For example, plead what was agreed; do not set out what was said.

Taking your own Legal Action

(4)   Unless they are very unlikely to be denied, such as the facts that an accident occurred on a certain date at a particular place and at an approximate time, try to use separate paragraphs for each allegation. This not only makes your claim clearer but helps the Defendant to draft his Defence succinctly. Remember you will want to be able to follow what he is saying.

(5)   Because a cause of action is based on setting out the essential facts, you neither need to nor should plead law, ie it is unnecessary to say that your "claim is for damages for negligence"!

(6)   Exceptionally, a point of law, which if raised or relied upon by way of Defence, not only can but should be pleaded, for example, if the Plaintiff's claim is "out of time" ie barred by the Limitation Act: "c" (above). It may also be appropriate to plead law in your **Reply**, which can "answer" the Defence: Form 7.

e: Remedies

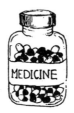

"REMEDIES"

At the end of your pleading there should be what is called the **prayer**, which is where you summarise what you hope to obtain. The usual remedy is **damages** (you will see from your perusal of sample pleadings that damages are either general or special) and **interest**. Other common remedies are **injunctions, delivery up, Mareva injunctions, Anton Piller orders, declarations** and **accounts**.

18

f: High Court or County Court

There are County Courts for each area of the country, although they do not correspond to counties or boroughs. For example, there are about 20 County Courts for the Greater London area alone. On the other hand, there is only one High Court (formally known as the "High Court of Justice"), although throughout the country there are many branches, known as "High Court District Registries", which operate from certain County Court offices. In the District Registries interlocutory work is carried out generally by District Judges, who also deal with County Court work.

Claims for damages for personal injury up to £1,000 or other claims for damages up to £3,000 are **"small claims"**, which are decided in the County Court: the procedure is by **"arbitration"**, which is basically that of the County Court but is more informal.

Personal injury claims for up to £50,000 should be started in the County Court, otherwise a claim may be started in either the High Court or the County Court, although there are provisions for **transfer by the court** from High Court to County Court or vice versa, which of course can cause some delay.

A personal injury case for over £50,000 or a case that is complex or involves a point of law of public importance is likely to be transferred from the County Court to the High Court. Conversely the High Court may well transfer a non-complex claim for under £30,000 to the County Court. The parties have a say in the matter before the court exercises its discretion.

If you choose the County Court, you can select any County Court in the land but the court staff will often send your papers to the County Court, within whose jurisdiction the Defendant resides; if not, his application for a transfer to his home court will usually succeed, unless all the witnesses are in your "area".

Taking your own Legal Action

Although the County Court has its own rules, known as the County Court Rules 1981 (which I shall call CCR), these tend to mirror those of the High Court, which are known as the Rules of the Supreme Court 1965 (which I shall call RSC). The CCR, being less comprehensive, are supplemented by the RSC.

The other major difference is that the High Court is "litigant driven", whereas the County Court is "court driven", ie in the High Court **you** issue the proceedings and apply for dates for applications yourself; in the County Court **you apply** to the Court but then wait for the **court to issue** your proceedings or to notify you of the hearing date of your application or the trial.

g: Letter before Action

"LETTER BEFORE ACTION"

Having satisfied yourself that you have a cause of action - preferably by having reached the stage of drafting it - it may well be that your opponent, the proposed Defendant, is actually willing to settle your claim. This may only be so in a small number of cases but, in any event, you should always write to the Defendant a **letter before action**, in which you seek an admission of liability - in personal injury cases in particular, it may not be possible at the outset to particularise all your losses - and/or ask him to refer your letter to his insurers or solicitors. You should in any event make it clear that you expect a reply within seven, ten or fourteen days, in default of which you will issue your proceedings. You may even enclose a copy of the draft "Statement of Claim" or "Particulars of Claim", which you propose to issue. You have nothing to lose by "giving away" your claim and may even convince the proposed Defendant that you mean business!

h: General Note

Remember that, if you are a Defendant and making a counterclaim, so far as the counterclaim is concerned you are a Plaintiff and should look at the relevant sections accordingly.

PART 2 - YOU THE PLAINTIFF IN THE HIGH COURT

1 - WITNESSES

Contrary to popular belief, cases are rarely won by pure advocacy. Cases are generally won by strong, clear and irrefutable evidence. Evidence consists of documents and witnesses.

First, although a witness may be called to authenticate, elaborate on or explain a document, a witness is generally called to give evidence of what he saw or heard.

Secondly, the importance of witnesses varies considerably. For example, he may simply have to confirm that he signed a receipt for payment, in which case it is probably unnecessary to approach him at an early stage.

On the other hand, a witness - preferably one who is independent - may be absolutely vital, eg to confirm the terms of a contract, which was made orally or to state - in an accident case - precisely what he saw and heard and how the cars were being driven etc or - in an assault case - who did what to whom, with what and how!

With regard to vital witnesses, it is, if not essential, highly desirable to obtain their evidence in the form of a letter or witness statement as soon as possible, as, however favourably disposed witnesses may be at the outset, their memories tend to fade and they frequently become reluctant to commit themselves or anxious not to be involved in litigation; like other human beings, witnesses may move away and sometimes "disappear" by becoming untraceable.

So, although **witnesses** will not give evidence unless and until the trial itself takes place, obtaining their evidence should probably be your first consideration. There is no rule as to how you obtain their evidence. This will depend on how well you know them. If they are friends, a telephone call coupled with a request for a letter or statement will probably "do the trick". If they are mere acquaintances, an approach by letter may be the most sensible way. If you anticipate any difficulty, there are many private investigators, who will for a modest fee obtain a statement for you in the proper form. It is difficult to generalise about the willingness of potential witnesses to assist. It is probably sensible, if there is any sign of reluctance, to appeal to their sense of justice and tell them that, if you were in their position, you would always be willing to help them by giving evidence.

In the last resort, you can force a witness to come to court by obtaining a writ of subpoena: see RSC Order 38, rules 14-19. There are basically two types of writ of subpoena: a writ of subpoena ad testificandum, which is for the purpose of them giving oral evidence; or a writ of subpoena duces tecum, which includes oral evidence but is also for the purpose of compelling them to produce documents (documents can include films and tape recordings).

Once you have obtained their evidence by letter or informal statement, it should be drafted into a **witness statement** in an acceptable form so that it may be **"exchanged"** at the appropriate stage of the case.

Virtually any attempt to suppress evidence - even by the lawful threat of proceedings - constitutes a criminal contempt of court punishable by imprisonment or fine: see Order 52, rule 1 and the notes thereto.

Expert witnesses

Possibly the usual expert witness will be a doctor or consultant, whose medical report or opinion will be required for a claim for damages for personal injuries. There will of course be many other types of expert witness. You may need a surveyor's report for a building dispute, a valuation of personal property, if someone has wrongfully taken it from you or if your insurance company repudiates its policy or an accountant's report to support your claim for loss of earnings. Those are just some examples of experts' reports; obviously there will be scope for reports from different kinds of expert in different kinds of case.

Taking your own Legal Action

2 - SETTLING YOUR CASE

It is assumed that you have drafted your claim and sent a letter before action: see d. and g. in Part I above and that you have been unsuccessful and therefore feel that you have to sue the other party by starting proceedings.

Nevertheless, you should always bear in mind not only the possibility but also the desirability of settling your case. Although you can never really know what the other party thinks, a true settlement is one where both parties are equally happy or equally unhappy about the settlement. In other words, both of you are accepting the possibility of not being 100% successful. Even where your claim is for a specified sum of money, the strength of the Defendant's potential defences may mean that you are not guaranteed to win. Even if you win, you may be unable to recover all your costs. Finally, a settlement will avoid the aggravation and anxiety of being involved in litigation, save your time and obviate the need to apply yourself to progressing your case through the judicial system and, most importantly, enable you to "get on with your life" or even "get a life"! In short, a bird in the hand is worth two in the bush!

Bear in mind that, whereas at the outset of your case, you are likely to be imbued with the desire to pursue a "just cause" and therefore full of enthusiasm, after six months of pursuing your just cause you may feel that you are no nearer your goal than at the outset and you may consequently start to lose heart. The same, of course, applies to the Defendant, who initially may be very obstinate. Gradually he will see that he cannot be as certain of resisting your claim as he first thought.

All this means that you should always be mindful of the possibility of a settlement. It is a fact of legal life that many cases are settled at the court door. Would it not have been better, if the parties, having been less courageous at the outset, were to have settled their disputes amicably by a sensible settlement? A settlement usually means each side giving up something. You, as Plaintiff, should not expect to obtain by settlement all you are claiming. Each party must make concessions. You must assume that you may not be 100% successful; the Defendant equally must, having made all due allowances for the extent of your claim, accept that his defences may not succeed. Both parties must consider the possibility of their witnesses "not coming up to proof" ie their evidence may be shaken or destroyed by doubts and/or skillful cross-examination.

Attempts to settle your case by negotiation may be undertaken orally or by correspondence. Genuine attempts to settle are "without prejudice" and unproduceable: see 18 - **DISCOVERY**. If done by letter, although unnecessary, it is usually marked "without prejudice" which covers all subsequent correspondence on negotiations. Simply heading a letter "without prejudice" will not mean that the letter cannot be produced in court, if the letter is not concerned with a genuine negotiation to settle.

The **golden rule** is that attempts to negotiate settlements should not cause you to delay the prosecuting of your case. Do not defer further action in your case simply because the Defendant writes, suggesting that no further action be taken until attempts to settle have been exhausted. There may be genuine exceptions to this rule, for example where you have both agreed that the outcome of the case will depend upon the report of an independent expert. Otherwise you should pursue your case avidly, even whilst you are equally avidly attempting to settle it, by two sets of correspondence, one "open", the other "without prejudice". Nothing concentrates the mind of the Defendant on reaching a settlement more than the knowledge that the Plaintiff is progressing his case to a trial!

Taking your own Legal Action

3 - STARTING PROCEEDINGS

Although there are certain forms of judicial process, which are started by originating summons, originating motion or petition, most claims will be begun by writ: RSC Order 5. Every writ must be in a prescribed form: RSC Order 6. Copies may be purchased from legal stationers or the Royal Courts of Justice in the Strand and an example of an endorsement will be found in Form 4.

4 - FEES

Although there are several types of legal process, which require the payment of a fee to "HM Paymaster General", who is, in effect, the "High Court's Bank", you are likely to be concerned with only a limited number of fees: these have just been increased and are: £120 to £500 for a writ, £30 for a summons to go before a Master of the Queen's Bench Division, £50 for a Judge, £50 for an appeal from a Master to the Judge in Chambers and £150 or (if for personal injuries) £500 for "setting down" your case for trial.

5 - ISSUE OF PROCEEDINGS

In theory there is a choice. You may **either** issue your writ, serve it on the Defendant (along with an acknowledgment of service of writ of summons form, which may also be purchased from legal stationers or the High Court), await receipt of the acknowledgment of service, in which the Defendant will generally notify you of his intention to defend, and **then** serve your Statement of Claim, **or** (short circuiting the process) issue your writ **endorsed with your Statement of Claim**, serve it on the Defendant along with the acknowledgment of service of writ of summons form and await receipt of the acknowledgment form **and** the Defendant's Defence or admission. Generally it will be preferable to follow the latter course.

Issuing your writ without it being endorsed with your Statement of Claim will, however, be sensible if -

(a)   Your are about to run out of time for starting proceedings (owing to the limitation period); or

(b)   You consider that the mere issue and service of a writ will be sufficient to achieve your objective or make the Defendant "pay up"; or

(c)   Your goal is to obtain an injunction. This would be the case where failure to act swiftly would be disastrous. Two examples will suffice: first, the Defendant may be threatening to build a structure which will either infringe your right to light or extend over your property, thereby constituting a trespass to land; secondly, he may be threatening to commit a breach of contract, which will result in irreparable loss unless he is prevented.

If you are successful in obtaining your injunction, then it is likely that any monetary compensation by way of damages would be of nominal value only. If, on the other hand, you were to be unsuccessful in obtaining an injunction, you may feel that no amount of monetary compensation would be satisfactory. In either case you will be able to save your time and trouble by not having to draft your Statement of Claim. To obtain an injunction, however, it is necessary either to issue a writ or undertake to do so.

(d)   You anticipate - possibly owing to not initially being in full possession of all the relevant facts - having to amend; it is easier to amend a separate Statement of Claim than a writ endorsed with a Statement of Claim.

6 - STATEMENT OF CLAIM

"Brevity, Clarity and Simplicity are the hallmarks of the Skilled Pleader": per Megarry V-C (1982) 1 All ER 336.

It is therefore assumed that you will start your action by the issue and service of a writ endorsed with your Statement of Claim. As stated above, the formal parts of the writ are prescribed and the forms themselves are readily obtainable, usually with sufficient space for your Statement of Claim to be written or typed. (Typing is obviously preferable, as it is clearer.)

Although non-compliance with small details - as in virtually every situation, for which rules have been laid down - can be dealt with or "corrected": see RSC Order 2, it is highly desirable that you try to obtain the Defendant's correct name and address. You should be aware that the terms "firm" and "company" are imprecise in their legal meanings. John Smith may be calling himself a company or a firm but, unless he is a partner in a firm or his company is a "PLC" or private limited company, he is simply an individual and should be sued as such. If there is a genuine partnership, you may sue the firm or any one or more of its partners because they are jointly and severally liable. If the Defendants are a company, their address for service will be their registered or principal office.

The Statement of Claim itself must (as stated in **d: Drafting your Claim**) set out the basic facts necessary to constitute a cause of action and provide proper **particulars** ie details in respect of particular facts. It should not contain a cause of action, which has not been mentioned in the Writ: RSC Order 18, rule 15. The need to particularise or provide particulars will vary according to the cause of action: see RSC Order 18, rule 12 and the notes thereto 18/12/3-21, which may be found in the White Book. As previously stated, each basic allegation should be set out in a separately numbered paragraph.

You may also raise points of law and amplify your cause of action by providing a narrative of background or subsidiary facts to clarify the basic cause of action.

Your Statement of Claim may also contain more than one cause of action provided each cause is against the same Defendant or Defendants: see RSC Order 15, rule 1.

If you intend to claim exemplary damages you must plead them in the **body** of your Statement of Claim, as well as in the **"prayer"**, which immediately follows the body of your claim and repeats or lists the remedies you seek: see Form 4. For "The Plaintiff's claim is for" **substitute** "And the Plaintiff claims".

It is convenient to mention here that the Defendant's response to your Statement of Claim is likely to be a Defence, possibly coupled with a Counterclaim, and maybe also a Request for Further and Better Particulars. If there is no Counterclaim, you **may** serve a Reply. If there is a Counterclaim, you **must** serve a Reply and Defence to Counterclaim. All these matters will be dealt with in due course.

The Statement of Claim will be the first **"pleading"**.

7 - SERVICE

Prior to service of the proceedings on the Defendant or Defendants, your writ or writ endorsed with your Statement of Claim must be issued.

What you need is -

(a)   The writ fee, which, as the court may not accept your cheque, should be in cash or by money order in favour of "HM Paymaster General"; and

(b)   As many copies of the writ or the writ endorsed with your Statement of Claim as there are Defendants plus one for the High Court and one for yourself.

Taking your own Legal Action

Then either post the above to "Action Department, Central Office, Royal Courts of Justice, Strand, London WC2A 2LL" or the local High Court District Registry with a covering letter saying "Please issue writ" or visit the Action Department, pay your fee and have it issued. The Action Department will endorse a receipt on one copy, which you will have to sign personally, and return the others to you, stamped with red seals. You must **retain** your copy stamped "**ORIGINAL**".

The next step is to type (or write) on the Acknowledgment of Service form (i) the **Case Number** (given to you by the Action Department), (ii) the **heading** (ie "In the High Court of Justice" etc) and (iii) the **title** ie the names of the parties (ie yourself and the Defendant(s)). If you use a word processor, retain these details in readiness for further use, which may be frequent.

Service itself is performed by you (handing personally or) sending by ordinary First Class post to each Defendant the sealed Writ and Acknowledgment of Writ of Summons form. Each Defendant will then himself or by his solicitors **complete** the Acknowledgment form and return it to the Central Office, which will in turn notify you.

If you started your action only with the issue and service of the writ, you must then serve on each Defendant a Statement of Claim at any time after service but before the expiration of 14 days from the time the Defendant gives notice of intention to defend: RSC Order 18, rule 1. If of course you have served a Writ indorsed with a Statement of Claim, it is then up to the Defendant to serve his Defence.

30

8 - JUDGMENT IN DEFAULT

Provided you have served your writ and the Defendant has either failed to return his Acknowledgment of Service form to the Court within the time allowed (15 days) or has returned it with a statement that he does not intend to contest the proceedings, you may, on proof of service by either your own affidavit or the production of the Defendant's or his solicitors' endorsement, accepting service, enter judgment in default. This is a purely administrative act carried out by you and the court staff; no judicial hearing by Master or Judge is necessary.

If your Writ has been endorsed with a claim for a "liquidated demand", which means a fixed sum, you may obtain what is called final judgment for that sum and fixed costs: Order 13 rule 1. If, however, the Writ is endorsed with a claim for unliquidated damages, which means that you have not specified the sum claimed and/or are claiming general damages, you may enter **interlocutory judgment**. This means that you have established liability and obtained your judgment but of course still have to have the amount of damages **assessed** by a separate hearing: Order 13, rule 2.

Similarly, if you have claimed in respect of wrongful detention of goods, you would be able to obtain (a) interlocutory judgment for return of your goods or their value to be assessed with costs **or** (b) interlocutory judgment for the value to be assessed with costs **or** (c) simply judgment for the return of the goods with no option for the alternative of paying for their value: Order 13, rule 3.

Where you have both liquidated and unliquidated claims, you may enter final and interlocutory judgment with damages to be assessed respectively against a Defendant, who fails to notify his intention to defend (and still proceed against the other Defendants): Order 13, rule 5.

Where you are claiming an injunction or an account (ie remedies other than damages or the return or value of wrongfully detained goods), you cannot obtain judgment in default, even though the Defendant has failed to give notice, but must proceed by serving a Statement of Claim in the normal way. If the Defendant fails to put in a Defence, you will then be able to obtain judgment in default (of Defence): Order 19, rule 7. Alternatively, you may elect to abandon your claims for an account or injunction and simply proceed to obtain final or interlocutory judgment as in rules 1, 2 or 3 of Order 13. Exceptionally where you have already obtained a Mareva Injunction, you may be able to obtain judgment in default **and** retain the injunction, if without it you would be unable to enforce your judgment: see note 13/6/1 in the White Book.

Finally, if the Defendant satisfies your claims so that you do not wish to proceed, you may take out a summons for the costs involved: Order 13, rules 6(2) and (3).

9 - SUMMARY JUDGMENT

"SUMMARY JUDGMENT"

Summary judgment is not dependent on the season but is perennial!

Although our system of justice is by no means perfect, it does recognise that in many cases the Plaintiff has a "cast iron" claim, to which there is no Defence. In these circumstances, to allow the Defendant a full-scale trial before a High Court Judge would not only waste judicial time and clutter the system but also, possibly more importantly, effectively deny real justice to such Plaintiffs.

These situations are catered for by **Order 14 Proceedings**, which permit you to obtain summary **ie speedy** judgment. This can be done where there is manifestly no Defence **either in fact or law** to your claim. It must be emphasised, however, that you should only try to obtain summary judgment where you are as sure as you can be that the Defendant has no Defence. Both the facts and the law must be clearly in your favour. If there are any grey areas of fact or even a reasonably arguable point of law, you will fail. The Order 14 procedure can be used for every type of action covered by this book except malicious prosecution and false imprisonment.

The procedure may be used whether you are claiming **damages, specific performance**, a **declaration** or an **injunction**, but in the last case the application must be made to a judge rather than to a Master, who is a kind of "junior judge", to whom most applications are made between the issue of proceedings and the actual trial itself.

It is most important to realise that you can only apply for summary judgment if (1) the Defendant has given notice to defend and (2) he has been served with a Statement of Claim (either separately or by way of endorsement on your writ).

The next step is either personally or by letter to issue a summons: see Forms 5A and 5B and pay the standard summons fee. You may apply under Order 14 "on the ground that the Defendant has no Defence to a claim included in the writ, or to a particular part of such a claim, or has no Defence to such a claim or part of it except as to the amount of any damages claimed": RSC Order 14, rule 1. When applying for the issue of the summons, you must prove, preferably by producing a copy of the Defendant's notice, that he intends to defend. Your summons must be supported by an affidavit: see Form 6.

An application for summary judgment may also be combined with an application for an **interim payment**, if appropriate: see RSC Order 29, rule 10(2). You may still proceed with your summons for summary judgment even if the Defendant serves his Defence at the same time as he gives notice of intention to defend or before issue or service of your summons, although in such circumstances you may find it difficult honestly to swear that there is no Defence.

If the Defendant has served a Defence and you still decide to proceed, the standard affidavit in support will be insufficient and you will have to add to your affidavit to show why the Defence, which has been served, cannot be substantiated. This is consistent with a litigant's duty, when seeking any remedy, to be candid and open with the court.

Thus you can apply for summary judgment on some or all of your claims or even merely parts of your claim and against one or more of the Defendants, making it clear both in your summons and affidavit with which parts you wish the Master to deal. Even if the Defendant has a **set-off** ie defence to part of your claim and/or a **counterclaim**, you may still proceed. For example, you may be claiming £20,000 and he may be saying that he owes only £15,000, in which case you may obtain summary judgment for £15,000, leaving the £5,000 to be subject to trial. Similarly, if the Defendant admits the whole of your claim but has a counterclaim which is **smaller** than your claim, you may still proceed. The summons and affidavit should be served in the usual way (ie by post) on the Defendant ten clear days before the **return day** ie day of the hearing.

If it is a complex summons, requiring more than 30 minutes, it will need a private room appointment. Therefore you should issue the summons without a date with a view to you and the Defendant seeking a mutually convenient time from the Master's secretary, who deals with listing.

10 - DELAY

"Justice delayed is justice denied."

As a litigant in person, your case can be affected by three sources of delay: the courts, the other party, his solicitors and/or possibly the Legal Aid Board.

If you need an injunction urgently, you may be able to obtain it either the same day or within two days (see **INJUNCTIONS** below). The High Court being "litigant driven", delay will result only from the length of the hearing and the relevant Master's available time. There are 10-minute, 20-minute and 30-minute lists. Only if you require ' nger ie have to obtain a private room appointment, are you likely to have to wait more than a month.

The principal cause of delay is the Defendant, his insurers and/or his solicitors. The Defendant or his representative will have two reasons for delay. First, they may genuinely need time to investigate, make enquiries of others, obtain and collate information and/or draft documents; such delay would be justifiable. Secondly, the Defendant or his advisers may simply wish to postpone the evil day in the hope that you will go away! Such delay is unjustifiable and you should take every **reasonable** step to avoid it. Although the normal time for each step in an action is 14 days, some steps eg the serving of a Defence, may reasonably require more than 14 days. Defendants and their advisers invariably ask for an extension ie "extra time"! Unless they provide a good reason, ask for one. In the absence of a good reason, take the next step, which may be to enter judgment by default or apply to debar from defending unless within, say 7 days, they comply with the rules: see **24 APPLICATIONS**. The sooner you react, the sooner they will comply and the sooner your case will be heard or settled.

Thirdly, the rules unfortunately enable the Defendant to make various applications, such as Requests for Further and Better Particulars, which unfortunately are often unnecessary and merely a time wasting ploy. There is no way of preventing this other than to try to ensure that sufficient particulars or details are given in your Statement of Claim or subsequent pleading.

Fourthly, if the Defendant informs you that he is applying for legal aid, you should make due allowance but there is no harm in you informing him or his advisers that they should apply for emergency legal aid.

Finally, if the Defendant enters into unnecessary correspondence, the solution is best dealt with by replying that you do not wish to litigate by correspondence.

Bear in mind only that (a) you should always act reasonably and (b) you yourself may at some later stage require an extension of time.

11 - CORRESPONDENCE

Obviously correspondence between the parties before action may be highly relevant. Apart from this, theoretically there should be no correspondence save for "without prejudice" letters and formal letters, serving and/or acknowledging service of case papers, ie pleadings, summonses, orders, affidavits, etc. For example,

"Dear Sir/Madam

Myself v John Smith

I thank you for your letter of 5 January 1997, enclosing Defence, service of which is acknowledged.

Yours faithfully"

If you have been unable by your letter before action or service of proceedings to obtain a settlement, you are unlikely to be able to do so by further correspondence. Unless it is relevant to the issues, further correspondence should be avoided. If the Defendant appears to be writing letters merely as a weapon of delay, a simple acknowledgment will suffice.

Having said this, it may be justified to confirm the grant of an extension of time or an agreement as to some procedural step. Many of the rules of court can be circumvented or dispensed with altogether by agreement between the parties. It may also be necessary to inform the Defendant that the matters raised will be dealt with "in due course" ie at the relevant stage of the proceedings or at the hearing itself. Too much of the wrong kind of correspondence could result in there being inconsistencies between what you write and either your case, as pleaded, or what you wrote in or before your letter of action. Therefore the least said, the better.

If you must write, be guided by the following "rules":

(a)   Be as succinct as is consistent with clarity;

(b)   Deal with matters chronologically and logically;

(c)   At the expense of brevity, restate what you are answering or dealing with so as to avoid repeated reference to other documents or letters ie try to ensure that each letter makes sense in itself;

(d)   Try to avoid the mere expression of an opinion, which does not call for an answer;

(e)   If in fact you do require an answer, make this clear or pose a question;

(f)   Unless the matter be a formal acknowledgment, ensure that you are not fobbed off with the answer "we are taking further instructions";

(g)   Do not allow yourself to be riled by letters from the Defendant or his solicitors, who are only doing their job;

(h)   Try to operate a follow-up system by seeking a reply, if you

Taking your own Legal Action

have not heard from the other party within seven days or such
period as may be appropriate; and

(i)   Remain calm, courteous and reasonable - never write anything,
which would embarrass you, were it to be read out in open
court!

To facilitate continuity and understanding of the correspondence, it is
good practice to start your letter: "Thank you for your letter of [date]."
or "Further to [my letter/our (telephone) conversation of [date],]..."

12 - ON RECEIPT OF DEFENCE

The Defendant should serve his Defence within 14 days from the
date of expiration of the time limited for acknowledging service of the
Writ or after service of the Statement of Claim, whichever is the later:
Order 18, rule 2. Thus if the Statement of Claim was endorsed on the
Writ, served with the Writ or served within 14 days of service of the
Writ, the Defendant will have 28 days from the day after you
served/posted the Writ.

The Defence should deal with all your material allegations by
admitting, not admitting or denying them. If the Defence admits an
allegation, the point is "won" and there will be no **issue** to be decided
by the judge, although you will have formally to include the allegation
in your witness statement. If the Defendant does "not admit" an
allegation, there will be an issue to be decided but it is likely to require
only formal evidence by you with or without documents. If, however,
the Defendant "denies" an allegation, there will definitely be an issue
to be proved by you, your witnesses and/or documents and it may well
be that he will seek in due course to **disprove** the allegation.

If the Defence fails properly to deal with your allegations or
includes irrelevant material, you may **apply to strike out**: see Order 18,
rule 19.

By reading the Defence in the light of your Statement of Claim, you can analyse which allegations are in issue and have to be decided. This will enable you to focus on the important aspects of the case, enable you to prepare for it and anticipate the outcome.

The Defence, may, "confess and avoid"; this means that the Defendant is admitting what you have alleged but asserting that it is irrelevant or does not, in the circumstances, help you to make out your claim. He may also admit the allegations of fact only to allege that they are of no effect as a matter of law. He may also make certain admissions but plead a **"set-off"**; this is a partial Defence: see 9 **SUMMARY JUDGMENT** above.

If the Defendant has neither "not admitted" nor "denied" an allegation, it is deemed to be admitted: Order 18, rule 13. By way of exception, however, the Defendant does not have to plead to damages or **"Particulars"**. Although the system of pleadings was intended to clarify the issues, there has grown up a style of pleading whereby the Defendant does "not admit" - **without stating any reason** - as much as possible. This has resulted in much delay, needless expense and, worst of all, obfuscation of the issues, thereby defeating the very purpose that the system of pleadings was intended to serve. It is hoped that the reform proposed by **Lord Woolf's "Access to Justice"** (that a party should state the reason for "not admitting") will improve the usefulness of pleadings and restore their role.

You in turn, may consider that you wish to admit or deny some of the new matters raised by the Defendant, in which case you should serve a Reply. If the Defendant serves a Defence and Counterclaim, you **must** serve a **Reply and Defence to Counterclaim** within 14 days. In either case, see the next section: 13 **FURTHER PLEADINGS**.

Unless you serve a Reply, there is an **implied joinder of issue** on the Defence: Order 18, rule 14, which means that battle is joined and you are deemed to have denied any new allegations of fact contained in the Defence. You may require **Further and Better Particulars** of the Defence.

13 - FURTHER PLEADINGS

As stated, you may wish to serve a Reply or have to serve a Reply and Defence to Counterclaim: see Form 7.

A Reply may be **desirable** to admit certain facts, thereby saving the unnecessary costs of proving them, to raise a point of law, to allege that the Defence has misunderstood the cause of action or to "set the record straight" with regard to new facts raised by the Defendant, which you believe you can overcome by further new facts. For example, the Defendant may have said in his Defence that it had been orally agreed that the written contract, admitted to have been made, was subject to a condition precedent that it was not to take effect until Mr X returned from abroad. In such a case your Reply would admit the oral agreement and then say that Mr X **had** returned from abroad eg by Concorde on 1 July 1996.

Even where there is no Counterclaim, exceptionally you may **have to serve** a Reply if, for example, the Defendant alleges that he performed or was released from the contract or that there has been fraud: for further details see Order 18, rules 3 & 8.

For the purpose of dealing with a Counterclaim, regard the Defendant as the Plaintiff and yourself as the Defendant and then decide in respect of each of his allegations, whether they should be admitted, not admitted or denied. The Counterclaim must itself constitute a proper cause of action and contain all the necessary ingredients of fact. It may arise from the same situation. For example, you may be suing for breach of contract of employment and the Defendant may be counterclaiming for non-payment of his salary. Alternatively, the Counterclaim could be totally separate. For example, you may be suing for money lent and the Defendant may be counterclaiming for the price of goods sold and delivered.

Remember, there is no joinder of issue on a Counterclaim; you **must** serve a Defence to Counterclaim otherwise you will be **deemed**

to have admitted the Counterclaim's allegations of fact and the Defendant will be able to obtain judgment by default.

There are yet further pleadings called **"Rejoinder"**, **"Surrejoinder"**, **"Rebutter"** and **"Surrebutter"**, all of which, save for a Rejoinder, are virtually unheard of and for service of which leave of the court is required: Order 18, rule 4.

14 - REQUESTS FOR FURTHER AND BETTER PARTICULARS

Although one of the cardinal rules of pleading: see **Part 1 The Claim (d): Drafting your Claim** is that you should set out the essential facts but not the evidence, you will remember from 6 **STATEMENT OF CLAIM** the need to provide proper particulars. In practice, if not impossible, it is exceedingly difficult to steer the middle course between **allegations** and **evidence** by sufficiently particularising. It is therefore very likely that a **Request for Further and Better Particulars of the Statement of Claim** will be served on you along with the Defence. This request may be justified or merely a delaying tactic.

As previously mentioned, you may wish to consider whether to request Further and Better Particulars of the Defence. What's sauce for the goose is sauce for the gander! The same rules apply to the Defendant's pleadings as to yours. For the practice, which is very detailed, see Order 18, rule 12 and the White Book's explanatory notes 18/12/1 to 18/12/26.

Having said that, it is worthwhile drawing your attention to certain general points and specific notes.

General points

(a)   Obviously if an allegation has been admitted, particulars cannot be requested: 18/12/3(6) *Admission*.

(b)   Generally one cannot apply for particulars of an allegation to be proved by yourself: 18/12/4(10) *Burden of Proof*.

Taking your own Legal Action

(c)   Particulars of special damages as opposed to general damages should be given: 18/12/6(21) *Damages*.

(d)   Surprisingly and notwithstanding the wording in rule 12(1)(b), if relying on the other party's knowledge, particulars of any specific facts, documents or overt acts showing that the party had knowledge should be given, if requested: 18/12/12(42) *Knowledge*.

(e)   The names of potential witnesses can be requested - not to ascertain evidence but to enable a party properly to prepare his case: 18/12/21(76) *Witnesses*.

(f)   Exceptionally you could be ordered to give particulars **prior** to the serving of a Defence, especially if the Defendant can convince the court that it is for the purpose of enabling him to consider making a **payment into court**: see below and Note 18/12/23 and you might even be able to obtain discovery of documents before serving your Statement of Claim: see 18/12/24(5) *Discovery*.

(g)   Do not imagine that the Defendant is not entitled to particulars because he must surely know the answer himself; whatever you suspect to be the state of his knowledge and however certain you may be that he already knows the answer, the rule is that he is entitled to know what your case **is** so as to enable him to meet it: 18/12/24(7) *Facts within applicant's own knowledge*.

(h)   If your Statement of Claim or other pleading contains something immaterial or what is simply explanatory narrative, you should not have to give particulars thereof: 18/12/24(8) *Immaterial averment*.

(i)   Frequently you may be unable to give precise particulars because of the formulation of the request, absence of detailed information (possibly prior to discovery and inspection) or because to do so would be excessively time-consuming:

18/12/25(9) *Inability to give.* In such a case you should answer: "The nature of the Plaintiff's case is that...".

Specific points

(a)   If you are claiming non-payment of goods sold and delivered, you must give proper details of the items of goods and when they were delivered: 18/12/8.

(b)   You also have to give particulars of **malice** (in its legal sense) and **misrepresentation**: 18/12/14 and of **negligence**: 18/12/15.

(c)   In building disputes, particulars as to defects are often ordered to be given in a **Scott Schedule**, which is done in a columnular form, with room for comments by each party and the judge and the prices charged and cost of remedying each defect.

(d)   In a personal injury claim, you should supply particulars of special damages ie loss of earnings, estimates of any future loss of earnings, expenses incurred for medical reports, estimates of future expenses and loss of pension rights: 18/12/22.

Whether particulars are ordered to be given will depend upon the Master, hearing the application. Masters (like judges) differ and have a wide discretion.

The accuracy of particulars is extremely important as, whereas pleadings may be readily amended at almost any time, including during the trial itself, you may be prevented from giving evidence, which **departs** ie deviates from particulars. Therefore you should consider amending or adding to particulars, previously given by you, which may be done by serving **voluntary particulars**.

When supplying particulars pursuant to a request or order, you should incorporate them as "**Answers**" in the original request, each answer following the specific request: see Form 8.

15 - AMENDMENTS

You may find that you either wish or have to amend your pleading, which you may do without leave (of the court): Order 20, rule 1 **provided** the pleadings (as opposed to any Further and Better Particulars) have not been **"closed"**. Pleadings are deemed to be closed 14 days after service of the Defence or Reply or, if there is a Counterclaim, after service of the (Reply and) Defence to Counterclaim: Order 18, rule 20.

You may also amend at any time with the written agreement of the other party: Order 20, rule 12.

It follows from the above that if the pleadings are closed or the other party will not consent, you have to seek leave from the court by applying by summons to the Master. The practice is set out in the Notes to Order 20, rules 5-8: see Notes 20/5-8/1 to 20/5-8/33. If you propose to amend your **Writ**, consult Order 20, rule 10.

The amended pleading is substituted in every respect for its predecessor save that it is deemed to bear the original date. This means that you cannot add a cause of action, which has arisen **since** the date of the Writ, although you can add amendments for the purpose of enlarging your remedy eg if the Defendant's wrongful act has resulted in further and/or continuing losses: 20/5-8/2.

Amendments may also be sought as a result of a change in the law or fresh information derived from discovery (see below). Provided the pleading could have been drafted at the original date in the way intended by the proposed amendment, leave will be granted despite the fact that the application is made after the expiration of any limitation period: 20/5-8/7.

Although leave is frequently opposed, the fundamental guiding principle is to allow the real issues to be decided and bona fide amendments will be allowed unless they would be unjust; they will not be unjust if the Defendant can be compensated by costs. This could result - in the case of a last-minute amendment - in you winning your case but having to pay all or most of the Defendant's costs.

As the court's role is that of umpire rather than inquisitor, it may "advise" an amendment but rarely exercises its right to order one.

Exceptionally an application for leave to amend may be made to the judge during the trial. This would generally occur where the evidence is different from what would have been expected by virtue of the pleadings. Generally, however, the application for leave to amend is made by summons to the Master, with the proposed amendment being set out, if short, in the body of the summons or by reference eg "as set out in red ink in the pleading annexed". You can, however, write to the Defendant, notifying him of your proposed amendment and that you will seek leave to do this at the trial; this would only be appropriate for minor amendments to correct say "Defendant" for "Plaintiff" or arithmetical mistakes.

The pleading should be marked at the top: "Amended pursuant to the order of Master   dated the   day of   19   ." First amendments are in red, subsequent amendments are in green, violet and yellow. The method is, using the original pleading, not actually to **omit** previous wording but (1) to put a line through the words to be omitted and (2) to add the fresh words using the appropriate colour; this may result in the paragraph numbers having to be amended.

It follows that if you amend your Statement of Claim, the Defendant will be entitled to amend his Defence, in which case leave to amend will be subject to you paying the Defendant "all costs of and occasioned by the amendment".

16 - ORGANIZATION

At this stage, you will probably have amassed quite a lot of documents. It is essential that you should be able to locate them quickly and conveniently, especially if you are "on your feet" in court.

Taking your own Legal Action

It will therefore be desirable, if not essential, to separate different classes of documents eg keep separate files for pleadings,

"ORGANISATION"

Further and Better Particulars, affidavits, summonses, orders from the court, open correspondence, "without prejudice" correspondence, letters or proofs of evidence from witnesses and reports from medical or other experts and, finally, legal authorities, extracts from cases or textbooks, ideas for future tactics, etc.

Finally, you may, having separated the various items, wish to keep a running chronology of significant events ie dates of service of documents, hearings and orders.

17 - INTERIM PAYMENTS

Doubtless on the basis that "justice delayed is justice denied" these rules are intended to alleviate any hardship you are likely to suffer between the time you issue your proceedings and the trial. They provide for interim payment of a proportion of the amount claimed where the court is satisfied that (a) the Defendant has admitted liability, (b) the Plaintiff has obtained interlocutory judgment with damages to be assessed or (c) the Plaintiff would **definitely succeed** rather than be **likely to succeed** in his claim, were it to proceed to trial: Order 29, rule 11(1). In personal injury cases, especially where it is necessary to see if over the course of time the victim is likely to make a full recovery or not, such orders are common, but can only be made against a person who is insured or is a public authority or is one whose means and resources are sufficient to enable him to make the interim payment: Order 29, rule 11(2). You cannot obtain an interim payment from the Motor Insurers' Bureau: 29/11/4.

If your claim is against two or more Defendants, the situation is more complex and you should consult note 29/11/2. For example, if your parked car was damaged as a result of an accident between two other cars and if, having sued both drivers/owners, they each deny liability, you would not, until the evidence has been heard, be able with certainty to say that both Defendants were liable and that either one of them should therefore make an interim payment; this is because one of the Defendants may be able to show that he was "innocent" or not negligent and that the other driver was 100% liable.

You may apply by summons (including an application for summary judgment under Order 14) at any time after the time for acknowledging service has expired: Order 29, rule 10(2).

The court can, however, if it thinks that the Defence is so weak or barely arguable, give leave to defend, conditional on there being a payment into court, which obviously is not the same as money in your own hands!

There must be an affidavit in support, which should verify the amount of damages, debt or other sum sought and exhibit any documentary evidence to be relied on: Order 29, rule 10. Your affidavit should also explain the cause of action and the stage reached and state whether you are claiming under (a), (b) or (c) of rule 11 above or pursuant to an account: Order 29, rule 12(a). Unless it is obvious from your pleadings, which should, if not referred to in your affidavit,

47

be available, you should explain why you will be likely to recover substantial damages. In a personal injuries case, you should additionally exhibit any medical reports and verify that the Defendant is insured, a public authority or someone who can afford to make the payment.

Normally the interim payment will be made to you but it can be ordered to be paid into court: Order 29, rule 13. Whether or not your application be successful, directions as to the further conduct of the action may be given as on a summons for directions: Order 29, rule 14. As in the case of a payment into court the fact that an interim payment has been made must not be disclosed until after the judge has decided on both liability and damages; consequently if a Master, when ordering an interim payment, gives further directions, the interim payment order should be drawn up and sealed as a separate order (so that the trial judge will see only the order for directions).

As to the **amount** of interim payment: see 29/11/5. Basically, in order to avoid the undesirable situation of the recipient of an interim payment being ordered to make repayment, which could happen, were the claim to be discontinued or where the sum finally awarded is less than the interim payment: see rule 17, the Master must exercise caution in deciding what proportion of the sum likely to be awarded should be ordered by way of interim payment. The rule does not **require** you to show a need but your own ability to repay the interim payment would be a factor in deciding the amount; so too would financial hardship or loss of income. In personal injury actions, however, it is customary to show a need, eg to pay for treatment, and the order can so state. Payment may be by instalments.

Interim payments and payments into court are separate concepts. There may be both interim payments and payments into court. An interim payment may, however, be paid from a payment into court. If, after an interim payment, a (further) payment into court is made, the Defendant should clarify in his Notice of Payment into Court whether or not he intends the interim payment to be taken into account: Order 29, rule 16.

To sum up, the court must be satisfied that you will on the balance of probabilities obtain judgment for a substantial sum by way of damages or account and, having done this, assess the amount of the interim payment by taking into account any set-off or counterclaim.

18 - DISCOVERY

In modern English "discovery", which is historically related to **Interrogatories**, means "disclosure" and now relates only to documents.

This obligation should not be confused with an **action for discovery**, which you may bring against innocent third parties, subject to you paying their costs, in order to obtain documents to assist you in a proposed action: see 24/1/2 and 24/1/4, without which documents you do not know whom to sue.

The obligation is to disclose all documents, which are or have been in your possession, custody or power and relate to an issue in the case whether favourable or adverse: **"Documents"** includes photocopies, data derived from computers, tape recordings, videos, etc.

The current rules for discovery are onerous, extremely costly and one of the principal causes of delay in bringing a case to trial. Thus it is good practice to prepare a list of the issues to see what is relevant and thereby eliminate unnecessary discovery: 24/2/5.

What is relevant includes documents between you and **third persons**, if they relate to the issues, eg a P45 from your former employer or an invoice from a printer. Discovery covers all documents even if they are no longer in your possession. Obviously if you have sent the Defendant a letter, it is no longer in your possession, although a copy of it is likely to be. Equally, as you have a right to get them back, you must discover documents within the possession of your agent or the custody of your servant or where you have a power (but not a right) to get them back.

You may be entitled to discovery of documents as a shareholder, member of a trade union or beneficiary under a trust; you may also be able to obtain an order for the preservation of certain documents in its widest sense: see Order 29, rule 2.

By now it may be apparent that the concept of discovery is merely one side of the coin, the reverse of which is the other party's right to learn what is in the documents. Thus there is implied into the act of making discovery the duty, without which the whole exercise would be pointless, to produce the documents to the other party. On the other hand the production of certain documents might make the administration of justice unworkable. Accordingly it is possible and usual to claim that certain documents, which you have nevertheless been obliged to discover, are privileged from production: these are documents protected by legal professional privilege, documents that might incriminate or expose you to a penalty and documents, which it would be contrary to public policy to produce, the main example of which is "without prejudice" documents. Thus you or the Defendant may be exempt from making discovery of incriminating documents.

Legal Professional Privilege is the principal category. Privilege attaches to all communications or documents that are directly or indirectly prepared or brought into existence for the purpose of conducting litigation, either contemplated or actual.

Privilege attaches to any communication for the purpose of litigation made to or by a party's solicitor. Where the document serves a dual purpose, then the dominant purpose must prevail. It is often difficult to decide the dominant purpose in the case of routine accident reports to employers or insurers. For example, where the dominant purpose for the report of an investigation of an accident was to avoid the recurrence of similar accidents, the report was not privileged, even though it could also be useful in anticipated litigation.

It is vital to appreciate that "privileged" is not synonymous with "confidential". Thus a letter from your doctor, confessor or even, so it has been held, a legal opinion from a former Lord Chancellor, however confidential, would not be privileged.

The right to privilege can be **forfeited** if it can be shown that the document was brought into existence to further a fraudulent or illegal purpose; this is not the case, where you have sought an opinion as to how you may lawfully avoid falling foul of the law.

Privilege, which is the right of the client not his adviser, may be **waived** or **lost**. Mere reference to a document does not result in loss of privilege as to its contents or other privileged documents. Once waived or lost, privilege cannot be reclaimed. Privilege is not waived or lost for civil proceedings, if it is a public duty to disclose what is clearly privileged in order to assist in a criminal investigation. If the other party obtains a privileged document by fraud or is even sent it by mistake, he can be prevented from using it or taking advantage of it to your detriment.

Originally privilege was confined to matters involving contemplated or pending litigation but it now also applies to any legal advice given confidentially.

Incriminating documents and those exposing a party to a penalty are privileged from production, although there are many statutory exceptions.

If **Privilege based on the Public Interest** is claimed, the test is not whether the documents are marked "secret", "confidential" or "state documents" but whether it is necessary for the proper functioning of government that the documents should be immune from production. Hopefully you will not be likely to be affected by such public interest immunity.

Within this category fall communications between husband and wife, information given for the purpose of obtaining legal aid and technical secrets but not information supplied on condition that it remains confidential.

Finally, no admission, however damning, whether written or verbal, may be divulged in court provided it forms part of a genuine attempt to settle your case. It need not contain an actual offer of settlement provided it is for the purpose of settlement or part of the negotiations: see 2 **SETTLING YOUR CASE**.

If, however, it is claimed that the case has been settled, the issue cannot be decided without looking at the "without prejudice" correspondence, in which case the documents are admissible.

If you believe the Defendant has not been frank and made full discovery, you can require him to verify that he has made full discovery by affidavit provided you do this before the summons for directions.

There is provision to obtain an order that the other party makes discovery and also that he verifies it by affidavit: Order 24, rule 3. Discovery by affidavit is generally conclusive. An application for a further and better list of documents may, however, be made if the list itself discloses or refers to other documents, or if the effect of the pleadings, the very nature of the case or surrounding circumstances would suggest a probability that there are other documents: see Order 24, rules 3 and 7 and notes thereto, which are somewhat complex and detailed.

Within 14 days of the close of pleadings, both parties must make discovery: Order 24, rule 2(1).

Although rule 2(1) is mandatory, one may apply to limit or postpone discovery: rule 2(5), and the rule is invariably honoured in the breach, there often being a tacit understanding to delay discovery until the service of any outstanding Further and Better Particulars.

Discovery is made by serving a list of all documents relevant to the issues in dispute. Order 24, rule 5 provides that the list of documents be in a certain form: see Form 9. Each document or category of documents (eg a book of receipts) should be listed in a convenient, usually chronological order with a brief description and a date in order to identify the document not divulge its contents. Failure to make discovery voluntarily or as a result of an order, may result in your action being dismissed or your defence being struck out: Order 24, rule 16.

Consistent with the concept that your opponent should not be taken by surprise and also with your duty not to mislead, making discovery is a **continuing obligation** so that you may have to serve a supplementary list, should further documents come into your possession eg concerning new employment, which could mitigate your claim for loss of earnings.

Having obtained documents from the other party's discovery, you are subject to an implied legal duty, breach of which could be restrained by injunction or treated as a contempt of court, not to use them for purposes of other actions than the current one, although there are exceptions to this rule, whereby you can obtain leave for that very purpose.

Special rules for discovery apply to motor accident cases (which are known as "running down actions"): Order 24, rule 2(2) and 24/2/6, to copyright actions: Order 104 and to claims for personal injuries: Order 24, rule 7A.

If the other party starts to drag his feet, you can apply for discovery: Order 24, rule 2(5)(a); on the other hand the court may decide that discovery **at that stage** is not necessary: Order 24, rule 2(5)(b).

It is hoped that new procedural rules on discovery - to be renamed **disclosure** - will be introduced pursuant to the reforms proposed by **Lord Woolf's "Access to Justice"** and that they will help all lawyers, whether they be professionals or litigants in person.

Taking your own Legal Action

19 - INSPECTION

"INSPECTION"

Inspection is discovery's twin. It means more or less what it appears to mean, namely looking at the other party's documents. Formerly this was done by physically visiting his premises and taking copies. Since the introduction of the photocopier, inspection is usually carried out by requesting photocopies. Thus you can write: "Kindly send me copies of Items 1, 3, 7-9, 14-20, etc from your list of documents.", such request implying an obligation to pay the other party's reasonable copying charges.

You will have noticed that the prescribed form for making discovery ends with a notice stating the time and place for inspection of documents. This is in compliance with Order 24, rule 9.

A party can inspect personally, by his agent or by requesting copies. As copies have to be paid for, if there is an extremely large number of documents, it may be prudent actually to read them in situ before requesting copies. Once inspection has taken place, it is too late for the other party to say that he included a document in his list of documents by mistake and forgot to claim that it was privileged from production. The privilege will have been lost.

If the other party fails to give the usual notice for inspection, objects to production or insists on an unreasonable time or place for inspection, you may apply for an order by summons supported by affidavit: Order 24, rule 11. Such application would be appropriate for resolving a dispute over whether a document is privileged. Failure to afford proper inspection voluntarily or as a result of an order may result in the action being dismissed or defence being struck out: Order 24, rule 16.

As you may inspect by an agent, it might be appropriate for your own expert to inspect, in which case he will be subject to a duty of confidentiality: 24/11/2.

Subject to the giving of the requisite notice at or before inspection, it is specifically provided by Order 24, rule 11A that the other party must within seven days supply requested copies along with an account of his charges.

Occasionally the court may be asked to decide whether a document listed should be produced: Order 24, rule 13, in which case it is up to the applicant, ie inspecting party, to show that the documents are not only relevant but also that their inspection is necessary for disposing of the case or saving costs: Order 24, rule 13.

If it would be inconvenient to produce an original book such as a business book needed by the other party, copies of the relevant entries, verified by affidavit may suffice. The affidavit should state whether there have been any alterations etc: Order 24, rule 14.

Unless the court orders to the contrary, all information obtained through inspection is to be used only for the purpose of proceedings until such time as it has been read out in open court: Order 24, rule 14A.

Although the normal time for inspection is after discovery, if you refer to a document in your Statement of Claim or in an affidavit, the Defendant can immediately notify you that he requires you to produce that document for inspection, in which event you must within four days invite him within the next seven days to inspect the document: Order 24, rule 10. Obviously the sensible course is simply to send him a copy. Equally, if the Defendant refers to a document in his Defence (or an affidavit), you have the same right. The purpose is to make it easier for the Defendant to draft his Defence or for you to draft any Reply; early inspection may also result in early settlement.

Whether you physically inspect documents or simply request and obtain copies of them, it is advisable carefully to read and scrutinise

Taking your own Legal Action

them as soon as practicable in order to satisfy yourself that the documents are genuine. This is because by Order 27, rule 4 you are deemed to admit their authenticity, unless within 21 days of the time for inspection you have so notified the other party. Do not confuse authenticity with agreement: you may accept that a document is authentic eg that it was written and sent but not accept that it sets out the truth.

So far as correspondence between you and the Defendant is concerned, your respective lists will be mirror copies ie you should have retained a copy of the letter you sent to him. Obviously there will generally be little point in requesting copies of **all** the documents, provided you are satisfied that you have the corresponding copy or original as the case may be. Occasionally, however, a party may - rashly - have marked his document, in which case, by requesting a copy of it you will be able to discover the way his mind was working at the relevant time. There may well be other types of document where you will want to see if the other party's copy is identical to your own.

" DIRECTIONS"

20 - DIRECTIONS

In theory you should issue and serve a Summons for Directions one month after the pleadings are closed, by which time - also in theory - any Further and Better Particulars requested should have been supplied, discovery made and inspection completed: Order 25, rule 1(1). This requirement may, however, be unnecessary where directions have already been given, in a personal injury case (where automatic directions apply) or in certain other instances, for which see Order 25, rule 1(2); in addition, the month's period may be extended by consent or will be extended by 14 days, if there has been an extension of time for compliance with any previous requirement such as an Order affecting the scope of discovery as in Order 24, rule 2.

The purpose is for the court and the parties to review the general state of the action and decide on what further specific directions, if any, are desirable. The Summons for Directions can deal with such matters as consolidating your action with other similar actions, transferring your case to the Official Referee or the County Court, any necessary amendments or further particulars, further discovery or inspection, administering interrogatories, exchanging witness statements, agreeing reports from expert witnesses or limiting the number of expert witnesses, defining and reducing the issues to be tried and deciding on directions for the trial, which include whether or not there should be a jury, trying to estimate the complexity and length of the trial and, finally, when it should be "set down" ie put into a list of cases, awaiting their turn for hearing; in certain circumstances, such as where witnesses have to come from abroad or medical or other experts have to give evidence, the date can actually be fixed.

In fact the rule that you should set down within a month of the close of pleadings is invariably impracticable, especially where - whether by mere delay or other legitimately obtained extensions of time - inspection has not been completed.

The Summons for Directions is in a standardised form (which may be bought): see Form 13 and is heard by the Master allotted to the case. Many of the items listed will either have been dealt with or will not be required, in which event you simply "amend" the form by diagonally deleting the **number** only of the irrelevant paragraph.

If you fail to take out the summons, the Defendant may do so and, if he does, he will almost certainly apply for an order to dismiss the action for want of prosecution: Order 25, rule 1(4). Unless, however, there has been intentional and blameworthy default or inexcusably lengthy delay, the Master will simply give directions. For what amounts to default and delay see Notes 25/1/5 and 6.

At the hearing, the Master should make all directions then possible and, if necessary, adjourn the summons for outstanding matters to be dealt with at a later stage: Order 25, rule 2. The Master will not, however, make further directions, if the parties agree or the Master decides that the case should be transferred to the County Court or the Official Referee, (who tends to deal with cases such as building disputes, where there has to be a consideration of detailed evidence), in which case directions will be given by the County Court judge or the Official Referee.

In order to save costs Order 25, rule 3 requires the Master to consider whether any of the strict rules of evidence may be relaxed by allowing certain facts to be proved by hearsay evidence or affidavit (or by use of notes of evidence from a coroner's inquest or from criminal proceedings): see 30 - **EVIDENCE**. He may also direct that there be a separate trial of a preliminary point of law, or certain preliminary issues or that the issue of liability and the assessment of damages be tried separately. He can direct that the papers that have to be submitted before trial should contain summaries of factual issues, propositions of law, legal authorities and/or a chronology of relevant events: Order 34, rule 10(2) and he will consider the estimated length of the trial and **categorise** it as an "A" (case of great substance, difficulty or public importance), "B" (case of substance or difficulty) or "C" (other cases).

It is particularly important for both you and the Master to consider whether your case should be transferred to a conveniently situated County Court, for which purpose the criteria are: (a) the value of the claim and/or the counterclaim, (b) whether the action is important to the parties or to the general public, (c) the complexity of the factual or legal issues and (d) whether, if transferred, there is likely to be an earlier hearing. A case is less likely to be transferred if the claim is for professional negligence, includes fraud or is against the police: 25/3/8.

If the parties make admissions, agreements as to the conduct of the trial or even an agreement not to appeal from the trial judge, the Master will note and direct accordingly: Order 25, rules 4 and 5.

In all these matters you will of course have a right to be heard and are expected to assist the Master.

A Summons for Directions adjourned without a new date being fixed may be restored, in theory, on two days' notice: Order 25, rule 2(7), although you will probably be lucky to obtain an appointment in less than three weeks.

Where the Summons for Directions has been adjourned, you may in effect amend your Requests for Directions by giving the other party notice seven days before the resumed hearing: Order 25, rule 7.

Even after the Summons for Directions has been heard, it may be restored in order to apply for further directions, if it can be justified in the light of fresh developments.

In **personal injury cases** (but not medical negligence cases where the ordinary rules apply: see Order 25, rule 8(5)(b)) the **Automatic Directions**, set out in Order 25, rule 8, apply and deal with (i) discovery, which is usually of a limited nature, (ii) the disclosure of expert evidence by way of written reports, which should, if possible, be agreed, (iii) the exchange of witness statements of witnesses who are intended to give oral evidence, (iv) photographs, (v) sketch plans, (vi) police accident report books and (vii) the category (see above). An application for directions appropriate in your particular case may be made, if not catered for by the Automatic Directions: Order 25, rule 8(3).

21 - PAYMENTS INTO COURT

Cynics, amongst whom may be found the majority of litigation lawyers, often proclaim that the law is a lottery! They mean simply that the outcome cannot be predicted with certainty. Logically therefore, if the result of a case cannot be known, it should be possible to bet on who will win and by how much. Ironically our legal system recognises this and the rules of court enable one legally to place a bet.

Unfortunately - as the rules presently stand - you, as the Plaintiff, cannot bet on the result but the Defendant can and would often be well advised to do so. Remember if a Counterclaim has been made against you, you are in the position of a Defendant and are accordingly permitted to indulge in this legal game of chance!

The making of a payment into court is one of the principal methods of settling a case. In practice, a payment into court is only possible where the claim is for "debt or damages" and only likely to be made where the claim is for damages as opposed to a specific sum. (In the latter case, because the claim will either succeed or fail, a payment into court is unlikely to achieve the desired effect and settlement is more likely to be reached by a simple **offer** of a lesser sum.)

To understand the importance of a payment into court and how it works, you have to understand the fundamental principle as to costs. Normally "costs follow the event" ie if you win, the Defendant will be ordered to pay your costs; if you are unsuccessful, you will have to pay the Defendant's costs. A payment into court, however, creates an exception to the general rule. Assume you and the Defendant believe that you will win and are likely to be awarded anything between £15,000 and £25,000. It is therefore in the Defendant's interest to pay into court an intermediate figure, such as £17,500 in the hope that you may be tempted to accept it. (This assumes that (a) he has the money and (b) he is not legally aided because the order for costs cannot be enforced against him without leave of the court: therefore you might have to wait for ever and a day until the Defendant's means become sufficient for you to obtain leave that the order be enforced.)

The judge is not informed that there has been a payment into court until after he has given judgment both as to liability and quantum of damages. The effect of the payment into court is that, if you recover more than £17,500, you will obtain all your costs but, if you recover £17,500 or less, the Defendant will obtain his costs from the time you were notified of the payment into court. On being notified of a payment into court, you must ask yourself whether or not you should accept it. Thus you are obliged to back your judgment, which may well cause you many anxious moments!

If you wish to accept the payment into court, which you should do normally within 21 days after you have been notified of it: Order 22, rule 3(1), you will be entitled to have the payment into court paid out to you, your action will be stayed and you will be entitled to your costs incurred up to the time you give notice of acceptance: Order 62, rule 5(4) plus the costs of applying for the payment into court to be paid to you: 22/5/3.

The situation is slightly more complex, where you have more than one cause of action. In such a case, the Defendant must make it clear as to which cause of action his payment into court relates, and, if it is in respect of several causes of action, how much in each case. You can then accept the payments into court in respect of one or more causes of action, in which case those particular causes will be stayed, and still proceed to trial on the outstanding causes of action.

A payment into court must be distinguished from a payment into court made by a Defendant who has, on an application for summary judgment under Order 14, been given leave to defend conditional on his lodging the sum ordered into court. A sum paid into court as a condition of leave to defend is there to abide the result of the trial and cannot be accepted by the Plaintiff, unless the Defendant gives notice that such payment is to be regarded as a "payment into court", in which event you are entitled to accept it in the normal way: Order 22, rule 8. This provision would also apply where the Defendant has paid the money to a third party: Order 25, rule 8(4).

22 - INTERROGATORIES

An interrogatory is a question relating to an issue. The answer to the question will either go some way towards resolving the issue or dispose of it completely. The purpose is thus to avoid calling unnecessary evidence or referring to documents, superseded by the answers, and thus save time during the trial, thereby reducing costs. Another way of explaining interrogatories is to liken them to cross-examination. There are, however, many questions that may be asked in cross-examination, which cannot be formulated as interrogatories, an example of which would be a question that goes solely to credit: Order 26, rule 1(3).

Do not be afraid to use this powerful weapon and try to frame interrogatories which support your case or destroy the Defendant's case.

Interrogatories, however, must relate to the case otherwise they may be disallowed as "fishing interrogatories". For example you cannot interrogate so as to introduce a new claim or destroy a Defence not being relied on, nor so as to found a cause of action or obtain evidence for another case, whether started or merely contemplated.

The right to use interrogatories is complicated by the potential conflict between two main concepts: resolving issues and saving costs. Thus an otherwise valid interrogatory might be disallowed because it would have to be answered by one, who would in any event have to come to court to give evidence.

Interrogatories will not be allowed where an answer cannot be obtained or is for a matter of opinion; nor if they are oppressive or cannot be answered without extensive investigation. They are also likely to be refused, if the other party is willing to volunteer further and better particulars or make admissions. On the other hand they may be allowed, even though the answers could and should have been obtained by a Request for Further Particulars.

You may interrogate about the general nature of an alleged

conversation although not so as to obtain the precise words. If the Defendant alleges he has made **payment**, you would be allowed to interrogate as to where and when it was made and the circumstances surrounding it. For the practice as to interrogatories on the **contents of documents** or whether someone has ever had documents in his possession see 26/1/12. This difficulty may, however, be circumvented by an application for specific discovery: Order 24, rule 7. As to what interrogatories may be allowed or disallowed in cases, where injuries have been caused by negligence, the practice again is complex and you should consider 26/1/13.

As they apply to "any matter in question" between the parties, the right to administer interrogatories between you and a third party or between two co-Defendants will not be automatic but will depend on the factual situation or state of the pleadings: 26/1/19.

When should interrogatories be administered? Rarely before Defence, if only because the issues will not by then have been defined. Just as discovery deals with documents and their contents, interrogatories deal with facts and the evidence in support of them. Thus historically they were associated and interrogatories, being derived from and forming a part of discovery, were formerly administered after inspection. The comparatively recent introduction, however, of the rule as to witness statements of proposed oral evidence having to be exchanged, coupled with the fact that interrogatories should only be allowed provided they save costs, has meant that the time for administering interrogatories has often been postponed until after the exchange of witness statements, which may make it unnecessary to administer interrogatories. This is unfortunate because of course the administering and answering of interrogatories may actually be a simpler and less costly process than the gathering, drafting and exchange of witness statements.

In short, no hard and fast rule can be laid down as to the timing of interrogatories and you must therefore carefully consider this interlocutory step, which is likely to depend upon the nature of your particular case. If in doubt, it is probably best to serve interrogatories and leave it to the Defendant to apply to the Master to have them disallowed or postponed: 26/1/21.

Should developments change, rather than apply for leave to amend your interrogatories, the best practice is probably to withdraw your original interrogatories and substitute a fresh set of interrogatories: 26/1/22.

For a precedent see Form 10. Remember that interrogatories are merely questions. Try to make your questions as simple as possible and answerable by a "yes" or "no". It is both possible and usual for there to be several questions, each set relating to one fact. The "second" question will often be "If the answer to the first interrogatory is "yes", what did the Defendant...?" followed by the third interrogatory, which will be "If the answer to the first interrogatory is "no", what did the Defendant....?". Thus gradually a complete picture as to the evidence surrounding a particular issue will be painted.

You must give not less than 28 days for the other party to answer the interrogatories, which he must do by affidavit.

Although they must be answered on oath, the Defendant or other party cannot limit his answer to his own knowledge; he is under a duty to make reasonable enquiries of others, especially in the case of a company, whose director or company secretary must make enquiry of its officers, servants or agents, and the answers will bind the party, whether he be an individual or a company: 26/2/2.

Remembering that interrogatories are part of and similar to discovery, avoid questions, the answers to which would not be allowed on the ground of privilege: see 18 **DISCOVERY**.

You may serve interrogatories twice without leave: Order 26, rule 3(1) but the other party may apply to the Master for them to be varied, postponed or disallowed: Order 26, rule 3(2). If you apply for leave, your proposed interrogatories should be attached to or served with your summons: Order 26, rule 4. The other party may put his objection in his answer: Order 26, rule 5(1) and should state his objection, whether on the ground of privilege or otherwise, in his answer: 26/5/2.

Thus any dispute, whether you apply for an order for leave to administer interrogatories or the Defendant objects to them, may be decided by application from you or the Defendant to the Master, who will take into account alternative methods of dealing with the questions eg by ordering further and better particulars, admissions, the production of further documents or exceptionally an oral examination: Order 26, rule 5(2); you can also seek further and better particulars of the answers given: Order 26, rule 5(3).

You can only go behind the Defendant's affidavit in answer, if it is manifestly untrue, to which end you may consider (i) his answers, such as they are, (ii) documents referred to or (iii) the nature of the case and facts surrounding the issue itself: 26/5/3.

Once again, the ultimate sanction for non-compliance with an order to answer interrogatories may be that the Defence (or, if the interrogatories are from the Defendant, the claim) will be struck out and that judgment be entered accordingly: Order 26, rule 6.

Having obtained the answers to your interrogatories, you may of course use them at the trial by putting some or all of them in evidence at the trial. If you put in only some of them, the judge may consider all the answers. Even though you are bound by the answers to the extent of not being able to go behind them or beyond them at the interlocutory stage: see 26/5/3, you may still be able to disprove the answers by calling evidence, contradicting them, at the trial - thus all is not lost by "unhelpful" or "adverse" answers!

You will see from this topic that it is highly desirable to gauge the strength of your case by reviewing the issues at each stage in the action, eg after defence, after discovery and inspection, after the exchange of witness statements and after perusal of the answers to interrogatories.

23 - ADMISSIONS

From your analysis of the pleadings, you will already have been able to see whether the Defendant has made any admissions. In addition to admitting an allegation in a pleading, the Defendant may write to you, admitting (the whole or more likely) a part of your case and vice versa: Order 27, rule 1.

Even if neither of you does this, a party may, within 21 days of the case having been set down for trial, serve a **Notice to Admit** any facts or any part of his case but only so far as the other party is concerned and **only for the purpose of the trial of their case**: Order 27, rule 2. Any admission made will be binding at trial or on appeal but not in any **subsequent** case between the same parties or against other parties. In short, a person may bind himself but not anyone else for the specific purpose of a particular case.

The purpose is again to save costs: see Order 62, rule 6(7). The effect of this rule is that, even were you to lose your case, you might not have to pay those costs relating to the hearing of evidence, which need not have been called, had an appropriate admission been made.

Remember, after any of the various stages, the issues that existed at the close of pleadings may have been considerably reduced. Therefore, you are again exhorted to review the state of your case at each stage.

Furthermore, admissions obtained as a result of the various interlocutory steps may be such as enable you either to renew or even to make for the first time an application for summary judgment: Order 27, rule 3 and Order 14 above.

You should carefully consider precisely what is being admitted; for example, the admission of a document as being authentic, does not mean that it is true. On the other hand, if the contents of the document indicate only one interpretation, which is favourable to you, you may be able to obtain judgment: 27/3/1.

As the Defendant may serve a Notice to Admit on you, you should exercise caution before conceding the point, as it might enable him to apply to have your claim dismissed.

It is worth noting that, in an action for damages for personal injuries, an admission of negligence is not the same as an admission of liability because, although the Defendant may admit that he was negligent, he may - as is frequently the case - deny that the injuries resulted from his negligence: to put this in legal terms, the effect of the Defendant's admission is merely to raise the question of causation or found an assertion that the damage was "too remote" ie was an unforeseeable consequence of his admitted negligence.

If for some reason the automatic provisions under rule 4 do not apply, you may within 21 days after you have set down your case for trial serve a notice requiring the other party to admit the authenticity of the documents specified in the notice and, unless he responds with a notice of non-admission, he is deemed to have admitted authenticity and likewise he may specifically serve a notice requiring you to produce the documents specified: Order 27, rule 5, which in effect makes the same provisions as in Order 27, rule 4.

24 - APPLICATIONS

As previously stated, the usual type of application is for an order that the Defendant should comply with whatever may be the next step in the proceedings within, say, 14, 21 or 28 days and that your costs be paid in any event. You can also ask for orders that, **unless he complies** with the substantive application sought, the Defendant be debarred from defending, and for judgment to be entered in your favour (and for any Counterclaim to be dismissed). The Master, however, will not usually make an "unless" order on the first application, but will probably do so, if he fails to comply with the first order.

It may well be that the Defendant has made sufficient admissions for you to obtain judgment, in which case an application may be made for judgment on the pleadings: see Order 27.

Even if you cannot apply for judgment, the Defendant's Defence may contain either inadequate or superfluous material, in which case you may be able to apply for an order to strike out his Defence or the superfluous parts of his Defence respectively: Order 18, rule 19.

You may use one summons for several applications, which could, though in theory inconsistent, be in the alternative, ie you may make an application to strike out or, alternatively, for Further and Better Particulars etc, in which event you would need only one summons fee and one hearing.

There are three types of application, namely (a) inter partes, which means that both sides are present at the hearing, (b) ex parte, which means that only the applicant is heard and (c) "opposed ex parte applications" which means that the applicant has applied ex parte but the other party has attended because he has either been notified or invited to attend or become aware of the applicant's application. This last type of application is usually where an applicant has applied for an ex parte injunction: see 29/1/8 and 27 **INJUNCTIONS**.

Although there are several applications that have to be made to a High Court Judge, the main one of which is for an injunction, most applications will be to the Master. They will be made by summons: Order 32, rule 1, which has been issued and sealed in the Central Office (or District Registry): Order 32, rule 2.

Allocation and Listing

Masters

The first time an application by summons is issued, other than a "time" summons, the case is "assigned", ie allotted, by the court to a particular Master: you have no right to choose your Master. The summons will be marked eg "Master Smith", to whom all subsequent applications must be made, unless the case is transferred by the Senior Master to another Master or to a deputy Master or placed in the floating list.

With regard to the hearing of your application, it will be given either a general listing or a private room appointment.

There is also a general list, which deals with short order 14 summonses, various other short summonses, summonses for directions (taken in the 11.30 list) and summonses for not more than 10 minutes.

For anything longer than 20 minutes, the applications are heard via the private room appointments list, by the assigned Master. These longer appointments are arranged after prior agreement with the other party as to estimated length and dates to be avoided: (see QB Masters Practice Direction No. 3 paragraph 20).

If you have to attend one of the short general list appointments, simply go to the Royal Courts of Justice, ask for "the Bear Garden" near to which you will find the court ushers, who will direct you to the appropriate room.

Judge

Inter partes applications to the judge will be put into the "general list", where 30 minutes hearing time is allowed, or the "list for special appointments" where (a) the parties agree that more than 30 minutes is necessary or (b) the judge has so directed because you have started to exceed the allotted time, when in the general list.

A Defendant may often suggest that your application will require more than 30 minutes. Unless you feel that he is doing so **solely** in order to delay matters, it is sensible to accept the situation and have the case re-listed for a special appointment otherwise you may well be stopped by the judge, and made responsible for the costs of the adjournment.

The matter does not, however, end there! If the application is listed for a special appointment, you should apply for a fixed date and the court will contact you and itself set a date for the hearing.

There is also the "expedited list". The above information about listing is referred to in 32/1-6/9 and further up to date information can be obtained from the Clerk to the Judge in Chambers.

Time for Service

Normally your summons must be served on the other party within 14 days of its issue and not less than 2 clear days before the date on which it is to be heard, accompanied by any evidence by affidavit in support: Order 32, rule 3.

For example, if the hearing is to be on Friday, you should post your summons on the Monday beforehand, so that the other party receives it on a Tuesday and has two clear days ie Wednesday and Thursday between service and hearing. Having said this, the other party may consent to short service or be willing to accept service of any or all documents by fax or you can apply ex parte for leave for short return.

Exceptionally, an application to extend or abridge ie shorten the length of time for complying with any particular rule - a **Time Summons** - may be served the day before the hearing: Order 32, rule 3. The other material exceptions are an application for summary judgment under Order 14 and/or an interim payment under Order 29, rule 10, and a summons for directions, which require 10 clear days and 14 clear days respectively between service and hearing.

Mode of Service

The summons (like any other document save one **requiring** personal service), may be served personally, by hand or by post on any weekday other than a bank holiday before 4pm: Order 65, rules 2 and 5.

What may happen

(a)   A summons may be adjourned generally, in which case it may be restored with two clear days' notice to the other party, or the Master may adjourn it to a fixed date; it may be adjourned as often as may be necessary: Order 32, rule 4.

If the summons is adjourned, it is the applicant's duty to have it relisted and to notify the other party, which is usually done by sending a photocopy of the summons, the original of which will have had the new time and date written on it by the court; such notification will of course be unnecessary if the other party was present when the Master fixed the time and date: 32/1/-6/19.

To avoid wasting the court's time and thereby depriving or delaying other litigants' appointments for hearings, if you wish to withdraw your application, the other party consents to it or you both agree to a further adjournment or that substantially less than the allotted time will be required, you should telephone or fax the Masters' Secretary's department accordingly: 32/1-6/20.

Where the Master has adjourned the summons for further consideration for, say 14 days, you may immediately apply for it to be restored within the specified period: this is because, were you to wait 14 days, you would not be able to get an immediate appointment: 32/1-6/22.

(b)   Although applications are heard in chambers, which are private, rather than in court, which is open to the public, they can be adjourned into court, if they deal with a point of sufficient importance or, if for any other reason such as publicity, it would be appropriate: Order 32, rule 13.

You must always retain the original of your summons, as it has to be produced to the Master or judge, who marks it with an often abbreviated note of his order; you will also need the original, as marked, for the purpose of the order being drawn up: 32/1-6/2.

If the **other party fails to attend** the first or any subsequent hearing, the Master may still hear your application and make an order provided he is satisfied that the other party has been properly served or notified of it having been restored for hearing: Order 32, rule 5(1) and (2) but he may direct that the order should not be drawn up immediately: 32/1-6/21.

Generally speaking, once an order has been drawn up and sealed it is "perfected" so that the application may not be reheard without the consent of the other party. There are, however, exceptions: 32/1-6/23. If you obtain an order in the absence of the other party, the application **may be reheard** before the order has been drawn up: Order 32, rule 5(3).

If **you fail to attend**, your application is likely to be dismissed but you may restore it for a rehearing, if you can give a good explanation for your non-attendance: Order 32, rule 5(4) even though the order has been drawn up: 32/1-6/24.

(c)   Note 32/1-6/5 contains a long list of most but not all the applications, which may be made ex parte to a judge or Master:

they are generally matters, where it is unnecessary for the other party to be heard. Consequently, if your case has proceeded normally, you will not be concerned with the list of possible ex parte applications.

It is particularly important, when applying ex parte, to disclose all the relevant facts. Failure to do so will make it easier for the other party to have the order set aside ex parte. You certainly should not risk a suggestion that you sought to deceive the court. Any order obtained ex parte, however, may be set aside by the other party either ex parte or as a result of an inter partes hearing (ie when both of you are present): Order, 32, rule 6, and any application to set aside an ex parte order should be made as soon as possible: 32/1-6/25.

As an ex parte order is "provisional", if and when the other party is heard, the Master or judge (whether the same person or not) is reviewing the order not hearing an appeal: 32/1-6/25.

The Master or judge may order an ex parte application to be made by summons so that the other party may be heard: 32/1-6/2. You may not apply ex parte simply because you wish to inform the judge or Master of information, which you regard as too confidential to be released to the other party: 32/1-6/2.

Unless directed to the contrary, no papers should be sent to the Master or lodged in court prior to the hearing: 32/1-6/2. Unfortunately neither the rules nor the notes thereto contain everything conceivably necessary to be known about procedure. In addition, there are nearly 50 Queen's Bench Masters' Practice Directions, which are set out in Volume 2 of the White Book and many practice directions made by the Lord Chief Justice, which are now collected in one section of Volume 2 of the White Book (although they are actually contained in the Law Reports). **Fortunately**, the vast majority of these directions are unlikely to concern you. You will also find that in the appropriate issue office, there is invariably at least one member of the court staff, who will be familiar with any particular rule of practice, which they will be only too ready to draw to your attention and with which they will happily help you to deal.

Hearings before the Judge in Chambers are also dealt with in 33 **APPEALS** and 27 **INJUNCTIONS**.

Where it has been decided that you will have a jury, you still make your applications to the Master before the case has been set down but to the judge after the case has been set down; if, however, you believe the Master would refer your application to the judge, you and the other party should refer the matter informally to the Master to decided who should hear the application: 32/1-6/10.

Although an application for an injunction must be made to a judge, a Master may grant an injunction if its terms are agreed by you and the other party: Order 32, rule 11.

A Master may refer an application to a judge, who may refer it back to the Master: Order 32, rule 12.

Practice Master (Queen's Bench Division only)

As previously mentioned, there is also a Practice Master on duty, who deals with ex parte applications such as consent orders and stays of execution, and provides advice as to procedure **without appointment**. You simply go to the particular Practice Master for the day between 10.30am and 1pm and 2.00 and 4.30pm and await your turn.

Senior Master

Should your application be urgent, it will be referred to the

Senior Master for a speedy hearing by whichever Master is available. Full details of the various Masters' lists are to be found in 32/11-13/4.

Judge

Exceptionally lengthy, complex or otherwise important applications may be heard by the judge himself, who also hears summonses after the case has been set down. If the judge adjourns the hearing into court: see rule 13, the hearing becomes public and may be reported: 32/11-13/5.

District Registry

If your case is in the District Registry, "Masters' Summonses" will be dealt with by District Judges or Assistant or Deputy District Judges. The powers of the District Judge are set out in Order 32, rules 23 and 24 under the sub-heading *IV District Registries*. District Judges were called District Registrars until 1 January 1991 and referred to as such in the RSC.

After the hearing

If you have obtained an order or have been awarded the costs of the application you have "the carriage of the summons" and you have to serve a copy of the sealed order on the other party. To do this, you should present the original summons, endorsed with the Master's note as to his order, and two copies of the order, one for the Action Department to retain and the other to be sealed and returned to you for retention and copying for service.

Save where the Master makes "No Order", all but a very few orders have to be drawn up: Order 42, rule 5. Orders are, however, effective from the moment they are pronounced: Order 42, rule 3.

Taking your own Legal Action

The best advice and safest course is to ask the Master at the end of the hearing whether it is necessary for the order to be drawn up.

The order should be drawn up within 7 days but, if it is not, the other party may draw it up: Order 42, rule 5(5).

The order is what the Master said and wrote - often in an abbreviated form - on your summons. You may well need help in interpreting what the Master has written (or scribbled)! For example, he may have written "P c i a e", which would stand for **Plaintiff's costs in any event!**

Drawing up the order requires the heading and title of the action to be set out followed by a short recital of who appeared, what affidavits, if any, were referred to and the actual orders made and/or directions given, utilising the type of wording used in the relevant rule rather than the abbreviated format, which the Master has used. Finally the order should state the date when it was made (not the date it is sent and presented for sealing). As it is easier to demonstrate by example than explanation, see Form 11A.

To avoid technical difficulties, draw up your order the same day, wherever possible: 42/5/2. If the order has been consensual, it should be drawn up "By consent" but this cannot be done unless the Master has endorsed "By consent" on the summons: (6) of Queens Bench Master's Practice Directions 30.

Note that Order 42, rule 5A, which deals with consent judgments and other QBD orders, does not apply to litigants in person: (5) thereof.

As a result of recent Practice Directions (on 28 October 1996) orders for interlocutory injunctions, Mareva injunctions and Anton Piller orders must be in the prescribed standard form.

25 - PLACE AND MODE OF TRIAL

The trial of your case will take place at the Royal Courts of Justice or in the appropriate court for the District Registry: Order 33, rule 1 and will be heard by a judge, judge and jury, judge and assessors, official referee, Master or Special Referee: Order 33, rule 2.

There are provisions for separating the trials of distinct issues and separating the trial of the issue of liability from the assessment of damages, especially where the working out or assessment of damages is complicated or, in a personal injury case, where the degree of recovery from injury is uncertain or where there are several actions based on the same accident eg the capsizing of a ferry. For further details, see the notes to Order 33. "Split trials" may also assist the Defendant to make offers of settlement after liability has been established.

Order 33, rule 5 and the notes thereto deal with jury trials, which, although you often read about them in the newspapers, are comparatively rare, as they are virtually confined to libel, slander, malicious prosecution, false imprisonment and fraud.

The outcome of a preliminary issue or split trial may of course be the dismissal of the action: Order 33, rule 7.

26 - SETTING DOWN

Your case should be set down for trial in accordance with the order made on the summons for directions, unless it is a personal injury action, in which case it should be automatically set down pursuant to Order 25, rule 8(1)(f) within six months from the close of pleadings.

To set your case down for trial, you should pay the setting down fee and lodge personally or by post a request that the action be set down for trial pursuant to the order in the summons for directions or in compliance with the automatic directions (personal injury action) and also lodge bundles of the relevant documents, which are called the "setting down" bundle. The rules are straightforward but too detailed to summarise and therefore you should consult note 34/3/2. The rules as to the keeping of different lists of cases are effectively the responsibility of the court officials: see Order 34, rules 4 & 5.

It is, however, **imperative** to notify the other party within 24 hours that you have set the case down and all parties must keep the listing officer informed of any settlement, likelihood of settlement, change in the estimated length of the case or acceptance of payment into court, as notice of acceptance is not automatically communicated to the listing officer: Order 34, rule 8.

Finally, it is the Plaintiff's responsibility to lodge two clear days before the trial two bundles containing (a) witness statements (which should already have been exchanged), (b) experts' reports, with an indication as to whether they have been agreed, (c) any documents requested by the Defendant, and, if having previously been ordered, (d) a summary of the issues, propositions of law, legal authorities and chronology of events: Order 34, rule 10.

Although this is referred to in the rules as "The Court Bundle", it is usually called the "Trial Bundle", the initial bundle being called the "Setting Down" bundle.

27 - INJUNCTIONS

Although you may apply for a **"final injunction"** before, at or after the trial: Order 29, rule 1, this section is concerned with what is called an **"interlocutory injunction"**. This is invariably applied for at the start of your case because it is necessary as a matter of urgency either to preserve an existing situation or to prevent a threatened action by the proposed Defendant.

Therefore it is frequently made **ex parte** on affidavit: Order 29, rule 1(2) and will usually be "negative" ie simply preventing the

Defendant from doing something; exceptionally it can be "mandatory", requiring something to be done by the Defendant. Even if you apply **ex parte**, you **may** notify the other party: see 24 - **APPLICATIONS**.

In **theory**, you must prepare a writ, with or without a statement of claim, a summons, an affidavit in support and a draft of the order sought; the writ and summons must be issued (but need not be served) and the affidavit sworn: Order 29, rule 1(3).

In **practice**, it is often so urgent, that a draft or unissued writ, draft affidavit or even statements as to their proposed contents and draft proposed order may be used in order to apply for and obtain an injunction, which must be drawn up and sealed. It can then be communicated orally to the Defendant or his solicitor and served as soon as possible.

To obtain an interlocutory injunction you must show that (a) you have a prima facie right, (b) there is a serious triable issue and (c) your right needs immediate protection; the judge will decide whether or not to exercise his discretion on the affidavit evidence without attempting to decide the validity of your claim but he will take into account the relative strengths of the parties' evidence: 29/1/2. This is particularly important where the whole gist of the action is to obtain an interlocutory injunction. This would be the case where damages would be an inadequate remedy or difficult or impossible to quantify.

Damages will not be a sufficient remedy if either you, the other party or both of you are unable to pay them.

Damages will rarely be appropriate, if the failure to grant an injunction were to result in irreparable damage to your business or reputation, the loss of a contract or market for your goods, the loss of your right to vote at a meeting, etc. The judge is more likely to grant an injunction if greater harm will result by refusing you an injunction than granting you one: 29/1/3.

You do not have to prove that the other party has already committed a wrong; it is sufficient if you can show that he intends to do

Taking your own Legal Action

so: this is called a **quia timet injunction** ie where "you fear" that a wrong will be committed.

Although it is possible to obtain a **mandatory injunction** - even ex parte - this would be most unusual and would require very strong and clear evidence in your favour. Were the Defendant to ignore the injunction or evade physical service, a mandatory injunction would then be more likely to be ordered: 29/1/5.

It is vital that the wording of every injunction is as precise as possible so as to enable the Defendant to know precisely what he must not do or what he must do. An exception to this practice would be in respect of the dissemination of confidential information or trade secrets, where too narrow a form of wording would enable the Defendant to escape compliance with the injunction: 29/1/6.

On applying, the judge will either refuse or grant your injunction, the terms of which you should attempt to draft before appearing before him.

He may defer his decision and order you to notify the other side immediately with a view to him hearing the application later that day, the next day or within some other short period. If he grants your application it will usually be for about 5 days with or without leave for the Defendant to apply for its setting aside or discharge within that time provided he gives you sufficient notice of his application.

When seeking an ex parte injunction, you must act promptly and show frankness with the court by not suppressing any relevant information, of which you are aware, including anything known by you of the Defendant's actions or intentions by virtue of conversations or letters: your own affidavit should deal with such information, including whether or not the Defendant has given notice of intention to defend: 29/1/8.

The Defendant has no right to apply ex parte in your case although he can apply for its discharge or variation ex parte (and can apply ex parte in a different cause of action of his own).

relate to the same matter provided he undertakes to counterclaim or issue a separate writ: 29/1/7.

If an injunction is one of the main purposes of your action, it should be endorsed on your writ: 29/1/9.

As stated, if you have applied for and obtained an injunction prior to issue of your writ and swearing of your affidavit, issue the writ first and then swear your affidavit (otherwise it would logically have to refer to a "proposed" action): 29/1/11. As in the case of most interlocutory applications, your affidavit may set out both matters within your own knowledge and matters of information and belief, provided you identify their source eg "that [Mr X/the Defendant himself] told you last Monday **and you believe**...": 29/1/11.

Where you have obtained an ex parte injunction, it frequently happens on the return day for the inter partes hearing, at which the injunction is either going to be continued or discharged, that the Defendant, either for want of time or for other reasons, offers an undertaking in the same or similar terms to the injunction. Provided you are willing to accept his undertaking, whether offered personally or by his legal representative, its effect is the same as if the injunction (as originally ordered or in the revised form of the undertaking) had been continued ie both your cross-undertaking as to damages and his undertaking subsist. Breach of his undertaking like breach of the injunction will constitute a contempt of court: 29/1/13 and 29/1/16.

If the Defendant obtains the discharge of your interlocutory injunction, he should ask the judge to decide not only whether the injunction was justly granted, even though there was no misrepresentation, lack of frankness or other delay on your part, but also whether he is entitled to an enquiry as to damages, which will normally be carried out by the Master: 29/1/14 and 15.

An injunction but not an undertaking, which is something voluntarily given as opposed to having been ordered, may be discharged

Taking your own Legal Action

if it be shown that it was founded on a wrong legal decision or non-existent legal right: 29/1/17.

Unless and until the application has been properly and fully heard inter partes, the Defendant should apply for its discharge, if he so wishes, to the judge; only thereafter should he appeal to the Court of Appeal, for which no leave to appeal is required.

The terms of an injunction: see Form 4 paragraph (4), invariably include words ordering or restraining "the Defendant by himself his servants or agents howsoever", which means that he cannot get round the injunction by using others to disobey it on his behalf.

An injunction, although it is only a piece of paper bearing the seal of the High Court, is thus an extremely powerful and important remedy.

Mareva Injunctions

Should you have reason to believe that the other party might evade the object of the proceedings, dispose of or dissipate his assets, forming either the subject matter of the proceedings or the source for satisfying any monetary judgment against him, you can apply for a Mareva injunction, which will freeze his assets, usually above a certain minimum amount. The principles and requirements are detailed and cannot be dealt with here but are contained in 29/1/20-35.

Preservation, Inspection and Samples

In addition to ordinary and Mareva injunctions, you may apply for an order that the subject matter of your action be detained or **preserved** for **inspection** or other purposes: Order 29, rule 2(1) and such an order may even authorise you to enter the other party's property: Order 29, rule 2(2).

A specific fund can be ordered to be paid into court: Order 29, rule 2(3).

All these applications require a summons to be **served**: Order 29, rule 2(5).

You may also obtain an order to obtain a **sample**: Order 29, rule 3 or for the sale of the subject matter, if it is perishable or likely to deteriorate: Order 29, rule 4. Property can include shares but not land or interests in or rights over land.

Your application could be limited to the taking of **photographs** or **photocopying** documents: 29/2-3/4.

Such applications should be made promptly by you at any time and by the Defendant after notice of intention to defend: 29/2-3/1.

Under Section 34 of the Supreme Court Act 1981, you can apply for various orders for inspections, preservation, taking of samples, etc in respect of property that may assist you in a proposed **personal injuries action**. This opportunity extends to persons other than proposed or actual defendants and is dealt with under Order 29, rule 7A and the notes thereto.

Delivery Up

By virtue of the **Torts (Interference with Goods) Act 1977**, rule 2A has been added to the rules, sub-paragraph (1) of which enables you to apply for the goods, the subject matter of your action, which may be jewellery etc, to be delivered up pending trial: Order 29, rule 2A(1). By Order 29, rule 2A(2) the whole machinery of rules (2) and (3) of rule 1 and the considerable practice developed from them and summarised above, applies to orders for delivery up.

Orders for delivery up differ from injunctions in two main ways, which may be advantageous. By referring to "subsequent proceedings", Section 4 contemplates an application for delivery up **without starting an action**, although it will usually follow. Secondly, the application

Taking your own Legal Action

may be made ex parte to the Practice Master, who is unlikely to order delivery up to you personally but more likely to order it to be delivered up to the court's appointee: 29/2-3/5.

The following guidelines apply:

(a)   There must be good evidence of the likely disposal of the property, which, if not prevented, would result in your judgment being useless, or evidence that the property has been wrongfully acquired;

(b)   The property in question must not be property personally used by the Defendant such as clothing, furniture, the tools of his trade or motor vehicles or goods used in his normal business;

(c)   The items must be adequately described or defined by you;

(d)   You will not be allowed to enter his property without the Defendant's permission;

(e)   The order for delivery up should not be to you personally;

(f)   Similar guidelines as in Mareva injunctions should be applied; and

(g)   There should always be liberty for the order to be varied or discharged: 29/2-3/5.

Anton Piller

Finally, an order for search and seizure may be sought to obtain evidence of infringement of copyright or the divulging of confidential information by former employees. The Defendant may refuse permission to enter but this would be severely frowned upon! This is called an Anton Piller order and is both important and potentially more intrusive than an injunction: see 29/2-3/6 to 8.

28 - DECLARATORY JUDGMENTS

The High Court has jurisdiction to make a declaration of right: Order 15, rule 16, even though none of the other more usual remedies (damages, injunction or an account) is claimed in the prayer to the Statement of Claim, provided the facts necessary for the court to adjudicate on the matter are sufficiently pleaded and proved. Although an interim declaration cannot be obtained pending the trial: 15/16/1 nor in default of compliance with the rules or by mere admissions or consent of the parties but only after proper argument before the court: 15/16/2, you may apply for a final declaration in **interlocutory proceedings** but this will only be very rarely granted: 15/16/7. You will not be able to obtain a declaration unless the Defendant has disputed your right nor where it would serve no useful purpose or be unenforceable eg in a foreign court: 15/16/6.

Although you will not be able to obtain a declaration on a hypothetical question, you may obtain a declaration as to the validity of a contract, ie whether or not it has been repudiated or still subsists, whether or not a restraint of trade (ie a contractual term preventing you from setting up on your own or being employed by someone else) is reasonable and binding, or whether certain rules or regulations amount to unlawful discrimination under anti-discriminatory acts of parliament: 15/16/2. For further examples: see 15/16/8.

If it is the only remedy you are claiming, the judge will be extremely cautious in exercising his discretion and probably not do so, where you are effectively seeking to use the declaration as a springboard for another substantive action: 15/16/3.

The sort of declaration discussed here should not be confused with declarations that are frequently made in judicial review proceedings; nor are we presently concerned with declarations as to status eg legitimacy or marriage, for which other statutory procedures exist: 15/16/4.

29 - SECURITY FOR COSTS

As an order for security for costs is only exceptionally available **to** you, as Plaintiff, **against** the Defendent, see **SECURITY FOR COSTS** in Part III, You the Defendant.

30 - EVIDENCE

Oral Evidence

The importance of witnesses was emphasised at the outset of this book, where the securing of their statements and attendance was discussed.

When your case comes to trial, you will, having made your opening speech, give evidence and call your witnesses to give evidence. All witnesses give evidence on oath or affirmation orally and generally in open court (but sometimes leave to adduce evidence by affidavit is given). Nowadays witness statements (signed and dated by the witness) have to be simultaneously exchanged. Such statements stand, subject to the judge's discretion, as examination in chief.

The law says that "there is no property in a witness", which means (a) that either party can call a witness and (b) that a witness cannot contract **not to give evidence**, such an agreement being contrary to public policy and therefore unenforceable: 38/1/2.

When the witness has taken the oath or affirmed that he will tell "the truth, the whole truth and nothing but the truth", he is "examined" by you, "cross-examined" by the other party or parties and "re-examined" by you, if necessary.

Examination

Subject to the judge's discretion, you may not ask your witness a **"leading question"** as to any issue in the case. A "leading question" is commonly believed to be equivalent to a "vital question"; this is a misconception. A leading question is simply one that suggests its own answer: for example, "Am I right in thinking that you saw the accident?" The correct approach - although extremely laborious - is as follows: "On Wednesday 1 January 1997 had you been to a New Years Eve party in Piccadilly?" "When you left, were you walking along Regent Street?" "Did you see or hear anything in particular?" If the witness goes off at a tangent, forgetting that he is meant to be giving evidence about the accident, the judge would not stop you from asking "Did you see or hear an accident?"

Alternatively you will doubtless be permitted to lead the witness to the important point by asking a leading question such as: "After you left a party in Piccadilly and were walking along Regent Street early in the morning of Wednesday 1 January 1997, did you witness an accident?" Thereafter you should endeavour to ask only non-leading questions.

If a witness - unlikely in a road traffic case other than him having jotted down on a piece of paper, the number of a car - made a contemporaneous note of his evidence, he is permitted to look at it in order to refresh his memory. **"Contemporaneous"** means at the time, shortly afterwards or even much later,provided that the event, described in his note, was still fresh in his mind.

Expert witnesses may refresh their memory by reference to a wider range of documents including professional literature, provided those documents can be looked at by the party, who wishes to cross-examine.

You may only ask witnesses to speak as to their own knowledge ie as to what they saw or heard, and not what they were told. The way round this is to ask: "Answer this question "Yes" or "No": "Did you speak to Smith?" When Smith replies in the affirmative ask: "As a result of what you were told, where did you go to....?".

If your witness fails to come up to proof ie does not give in evidence what he said in his statement or becomes **"hostile"** by resiling from what he told you he was going to say, the judge will doubtless allow you to show the witness his original letter or statement and, provided he admits that he signed the statement, you will be allowed to put to him that he earlier on gave a different version, consistent with your case. This may not, however, help you, as the judge is unlikely to attach much weight to that witness. You may of course have another witness, who can deal with the same point, over which the first witness was hostile.

Cross-examination

"Cross examination" does not mean "examine crossly"! When cross examining, you may ask leading questions, suggest to the witness the answer you seek, put to him that he is mistaken or untruthful. You are not limited to the matters, on which he was examined in chief by the person who called him, but may ask any relevant question, including questions designed to undermine his credibility. If, however, you do so, you are then bound by his answer unless it relates to the denial of a criminal conviction. You may seek to show that he is biased and/or that he has previously made inconsistent statements. If the previously made inconsistent statements are in writing, they should be shown to him to give him a fair opportunity to reconsider his evidence.Subject to the judge's discretion, he is not obliged to answer in a way that will incriminate him or expose him to a penalty.

A third party or co-defendant will not be entitled to cross examine, unless the evidence affects issues relevant to his own Defence or case.

Re-examination

At the end of the cross-examination by the other party or parties, you will be allowed to re-examine your witness not for the purpose of restating his evidence but to explain matters that arose from cross-examination. Without the judge's leave, you will not be allowed to include in your re-examination a question that you should have asked in examination in chief. Re-examination must be on a point that **arises from cross-examination**.

Unlike criminal trials, witnesses are allowed to be in court before they give evidence. Exceptionally - where you consider the likelihood of collusion - you may ask that witnesses be kept out of court until they have given evidence and also, after they have given evidence, to leave without communicating with other witnesses yet to be called.

The judge himself may call a witness and examine him. If so, although there is no **right** to cross-examine, you will normally be permitted to do so: 38/1/7.

If the Defendant has called evidence on a particular issue, which he had a duty to prove, the judge is likely to allow you to call evidence to **rebut** ie contradict the witness's evidence even though the nature of that evidence was apparent from his cross-examination of your witnesses. So too may you call evidence in rebuttal where there has been contradictory evidence or you have been taken by surprise: 38/1/8.

Sundry Points

After judgment has been given, the only evidence permissible will be evidence as to "without prejudice" offers as to costs: 38/1/10.

If the authenticity of a deed or documents is disputed, its authenticity can be proved by the party who made it, attested, ie witnessed, it or a person familiar with the maker's handwriting: 38/1/11.

Taking your own Legal Action

Whether an answer is incriminating, depends not on the witness's own belief but the view of the judge: 38/1/13.

Tape recordings and videos are admissible evidence. As to evidence from other proceedings: see the Civil Evidence Act 1968 Section 4.

Affidavit Evidence

With regard to an affidavit sworn before an action has been issued, it should correctly refer to an "intended action": 41/1/3.

Although affidavit evidence may be used in applications, such affidavits may not be used at the trial without the leave of the court. An application for leave, though it may be made at the trial, is usually made on the summons for directions. This will be useful if the maker of the affidavit is abroad or where the contents are unlikely to be disputed. The other party has a right to see the affidavit proposed to be used or to be informed of the nature of its contents. It is, however, unlikely that leave will be given, where the contents of the affidavit relate to a vital and disputed issue: 38/2/1.

If you do obtain leave to use the affidavit, the other party may rely on any admissions made in it: 38/2/6.

The judge may well refuse to accept the effect of the affidavit where the other party is unable to cross-examine the deponent (ie maker of the affidavit): 38/2/6.

It is also possible for the other party to obtain an order to cross-examine the maker who is resident abroad: 38/2/6. In deciding whether or not there should be cross-examination, the deponent's motive and bona fides will be relevant: 38/2/6.

The Rules for Affidavits

These are to be found in Order 41, which incorporates a Practice Direction made by the Lord Chief Justice on July 21, 1983: see 41/11/1 (which is worth reading).

The affidavit should be marked at the top right corner: see Form 12 and be followed by the heading and (summarised) title of the action, state the deponent's capacity and his private or business address. It should be made in the first person (singular or plural): Order 41, rule 1.

An affidavit should be confined to facts within the deponent's own knowledge, subject to the important exceptions, which are when it is made for the purpose of an application for summary judgment under Order 14, interlocutory applications generally or pursuant to Order 32, rule 3 (see below under *Hearsay Evidence*): Order 41, rule 5.

Try to draft it as succinctly as is consistent with clarity, since, like pleadings, parts or all of it may be struck out, if it is scandalous, irrelevant or oppressive: Order 41, rule 6, in respect of which similar considerations apply as under Order 18, rule 19 (striking out).

An affidavit may be written, typed or even printed on either one or both sides of A4 paper, which should be numbered. The contents should be divided into numbered paragraphs (like pleadings); use numbers not words. It has to be sworn or affirmed: see generally Order 41, rule 1.

An affidavit may be made jointly by two or more deponents: Order 41, rule 2 or by an illiterate or blind person: Order 41, rule 3.

Alterations after drafting have to be initialled at the time of swearing or affirmation: Order 41, rule 7 otherwise they may have to be resworn.

Despite Order 41, rule 9, which requires **the original affidavit** to be filed in the District Registry, the Supreme Court Taxing Office or

Taking your own Legal Action

(if in the High Court) with the Filing and Record Department of the Central Office, the usual practice is for you to give it to the Master, judge or his clerk at the hearing of your interlocutory application, after which it is filed by the court: 41/10/1. Therefore you should always **keep a copy** for yourself. If it is required at a later hearing, it must be **"bespoken"** ie you must ask the relevant office to produce it for the hearing: 41/9/2.

    Exhibits should also be marked. They may contain copies, provided the originals are available for inspection before or at the hearing.

    Affidavits and exhibits should be bound up: the correct method is by ribbon, tied in a knot and sealed, not with plastic strips: 41/1/9; stapling is **theoretically** unacceptable but frequent in practice.

    Although it is meant to be "bound in book form": Order 41, rule 1(5) this and any other formal irregularity may be dispensed with, for which leave may be obtained ex parte: Order 41, rule 4.

    Exhibits, which must also be properly bound or secured, must not be attached to the affidavit and, after any hearing, are returned for retention by the party relying on them.

    Letters should be contained, if possible, in one bundle in chronological order with consecutive numbering at centre bottom.

    With regard to exhibits other than documents, the principle is simply to ensure that they are readily identifiable by marking them or by attaching to them an appropriately marked slip. If too small, they should be enclosed in a sealed transparent container.

    Do not exhibit but simply refer to pleadings, your own previous affidavit or the other party's affidavit.

    If you have only one exhibit, it will be marked with your initials eg "AB"; if your first affidavit contains more than one exhibit, the first exhibit will be marked "AB1"; further exhibits in the same or subsequent affidavits should be marked "AB2", "AB3", etc. Thus if your first three affidavits contain ten exhibits, the first exhibit in your fourth affidavit will be "AB11"; thus confusion between exhibits will be avoided as each one will have an unique number.

Prerequisites

The summons for directions should include directions for parties to serve on each other written statements of the oral evidence they intend to call in relation to the issues: see Order 38, rule 2A, which is a comparatively new order - formerly witness statements did not have to be exchanged - and which contains all the information necessary as to the requirements of such written statements, such as their dating and inclusion of the fact that they are true (however obvious this may be).

The introduction of this rule was an extension of openness in litigation and also for the purpose of bringing about settlements - after due consideration of the case - without having to proceed to trial. It was also intended to result in admissions and reduce cross-examination: 38/2A/2.

If one or more parties wishes to serve witness statements, they are meant to be "exchanged simultaneously". This of course is subject to a party's ability to obtain a witness statement: see 1 **WITNESSES**, which deals with witnesses, who will not come to court voluntarily.

Non-compliance with these stringent rules will prevent you from calling the evidence without the court's leave. The courts may vary directions but not admit inadmissible evidence: Order 38, rule 2A(8).

It is important that the witness clearly identifies any documents referred to: Order 38, rule 2A(4)(b).

As the statement should not anticipate opponents' statements or cross-examination, it may be subject to an application for amendment: 38/2A/9 or result in a supplementary statement being ordered: 38/2A/10.

The witness's statement itself remains confidential and is not evidence unless and until he is called to give evidence. Unless the witness statement is ordered to stand as the examination in chief, you must still adduce the evidence by non-leading questions; the other party retains the right to cross-examine: 38/2A/11.

Unlike affidavits, witness statements should not contain hearsay evidence ie what the witness was told by others nor, unless he is an expert witness, his opinion: 38/2A/12.

Expert Evidence

At the summons for directions the Master will usually order that experts' reports be exchanged and, if possible, agreed, in default of which the number of expert witnesses should be limited usually to two witnesses per party in each area of expertise eg two medical witnesses, one engineer's report, one structural surveyor's report, one accountant's report, etc. It sometimes occurs that witnesses of fact are also expert in the particular field in question but they do not rank as "experts": 38/4/1 as it would not be right, where a party's witness of fact is also an expert, to prevent that party from calling an **independent** expert: 38/4/2.

It is important to understand that an expert is there to assist the court in the understanding of a technical, medical or other process **not** to decide the case; this remains the province of the judge (and jury): 38/4/2.

As experts are not subject to the hearsay rule of evidence, they may rely on the research, statistics, materials etc of others: 38/4/2.

A person who has knowledge of the laws of a foreign jurisdiction is regarded as an expert witness. His opinion of the law of that other country is, however, a matter of fact. Like the evidence of any other expert, it need not be accepted by the court.

It is worth noting that even handwriting is an area of expertise, which means that the judge himself cannot decide on the question of disputed handwriting or signature without hearing expert evidence.

Note that Order 40 of the Rules specifically provides for the **appointment of an expert by the court**. A court expert may be appointed on the application of one party or by agreement and may be selected, if not by the agreement of the parties, by the court: Order 40, rule 1. A court expert is still subject to cross-examination: Order 40, rule 4 and his report does not prevent either party from calling his own expert: Order 40, rule 6. If you do not know what an expert will say, a court expert will save you costs.

You cannot call an expert witness to give oral evidence unless (a) the court has given leave, (b) the other parties consent, (c) you have complied with a previously obtained direction as to advance disclosure of the nature of the evidence or (d) you have complied with the personal injuries automatic directions.

For expert **oral** evidence see rule 37; for expert **written** evidence see rule 41. These matters should have been considered on the summons for directions: Order 25, rule 3. See Section 20 **DIRECTIONS**.

Another useful provision is for there to be a "without prejudice" meeting of the experts before or after their reports have been exchanged so that the experts may assist the case generally by setting out those points on which they agree and disagree: Order 38, rule 38.

It follows that, if there has been no direction to exchange reports or only to exchange certain parts of them, the party is free to call his expert to give evidence: Order 38, rule 39.

In short, although expert evidence is generally directed to be exchanged simultaneously by written report or affidavit, a departure from this practice will still leave you free to call your expert witness to give oral evidence: 38/37-39/1. This applies, with the exception of the initial medical report served with the statement of claim, to subsequent medical reports in personal injuries cases: 38/37-39/2.

Taking your own Legal Action

Obviously the court cannot consider whether only part of an expert's report should be disclosed: 38/37-39/5 without exercising its power to see the document under Order 24, rule 12.

If the court directs all the experts to meet, anything agreed ceases to be "without prejudice": 36/37-39/6, the whole point of the exercise being to limit the issues, thus shortening the length of the trial.

Although your expert cannot bind you without authority, as a matter of common sense he will find it difficult to give evidence inconsistent with something he has agreed with the opposite party's expert.

You may include in your own case the disclosed report of the other party's expert: Order 38, rule 42. He will then be liable to cross-examination.

If an expert's report has been disclosed under Order 37, it is generally put in prior to or during examination in chief: Order 38, rule 43.

Finally, any direction may be withdrawn or varied by the court for good cause: Order 38, rule 44.

Plans etc

Plans, photographs, models etc may also be put in evidence subject to inspection and may be agreed or admitted: Order 38, rule 5.

Hearsay Evidence

Put shortly, hearsay evidence is evidence of what the witness was told by another person or evidence based on records kept by another or facts derived from a computer, of which the witness has no personal knowledge.

Hearsay evidence is dealt with in Part III of Order 38 by rules 20-34, which have been added pursuant to Sections 1-10 of the Civil

Evidence Act 1968. A useful summary of the section may be found in 38/20/1 and 2.

If you wish to use hearsay evidence, you should within 21 days of the case being set down for trial or hearing or within such other period as the court may order **serve** on all other parties a **notice** (for which there is no prescribed form) specifying that you intend to adduce hearsay evidence: Order 38, rule 21.

The notice should contain details of the time, place and circumstances in which the statement was made, by and to whom and the substance of the statement: Order 38, rule 22(1). If the statement is comprised in a document, a copy of it should be served with the notice: Order 38, rule 22(2).

If the maker of the statement (a) has died, (b) is abroad, (c) is physically or mentally unfit to give evidence, (d) cannot be identified or found despite your reasonable efforts or (e) cannot be expected to remember what he has said: see Order 38, rule 25, you should state this in your notice: Order 38, rule 22(3).

The same requirements apply in respect of statements, containing the making of certain records compiled by other persons, who might be said to be acting in the normal course of their occupation: Order 38, rule 23 and to statements, which include what may loosely be described as computerised information: Order 38, rule 24. The statements and/or information, covered by these two rules, are defined by Sections 4 and 5 respectively of the Civil Evidence Act. It is immaterial whether the original maker or compiler of the statement was in paid employment or not. It is intended to avoid the calling of persons, making routine records, who would not be likely to have had any reason to suppress or distort their records.

The purpose of this part of the rules of court is twofold: first, to save the unnecessary calling of witnesses and secondly, to ensure that due weight may be given to statements of persons, whom it is impossible or impracticable to call. In respect of impossibility or impracticability, any one of the five reasons is sufficient eg, if the maker of the statement is abroad, it is unnecessary to show that you have asked him voluntarily to attend t he trial: 38/22-25/3.

On service of the notice, the other party or parties may serve a **counter-notice** within 21 days, requiring you to call the witness: Order 38, rule 26, stating, if it be the case, that the person **can** or **should** be called to give evidence: Order 38, rule 26(2). If you receive such a counter-notice, you have to call the witness subject to leave under Order 38, rule 29 being granted by the court for the statement to be used in court.

Once again any issue raised by the notice and counter-notice may be decided by the Master on application, for which see rules 27 and 28.

Unless the counter-notice is challenged or over-ruled by the discretion of the court under rule 29, the other party will be able to prevent you from making use at the trial of oral or written statements made by witnesses not being called or evidence contained in records or derived from computers: 38/26/2.

Whether or not any of the reasons in rule 25 apply to a particular witness should be decided before the hearing but the question can be raised again at the trial if the cir cumstances have changed eg by the recovery of a sick person or a person going abroad: Order 38, rule 27.

Rule 28 makes provision for admitting evidence, originally heard in previous civil or criminal proceedings, or the effect of it, being admitted by way of hearsay evidence.

Rule 29 is a saving rule and still enables you or the other party to apply to admit or prevent hearsay evidence, even though the strict procedural rules have not been complied with, if it would be just to do so. What weight be given to hearsay evidence is another question. This may well depend on both its nature, whether it is crucial and the fact that it cannot be tested by cross-examination. The court will always take into consideration the obvious undesirability of forcing you to call the other party or his servant or agent as your own witness: 38/29/1.

If an oral statement is tape recorded without the knowledge of the speaker, it has to be proved by the speaker or someone who heard him. If, however, the speaker knew that his statement was being recorded, such statement is deemed to be a document: 38/29/1.

Whether or not all the notices or counter-notices have been served, it is still possible for the credibility of the hearsay witness to be impugned: Order 38, rule 30. It is also possible to show that a hearsay witness has made inconsistent statements: Order 38, rule 31. Rule 32 provides for costs to be paid by a party, who is found to have unreasonably served a counter-notice, but does not deprive the court of its general discretion as to costs: see 34 **COSTS**.

Rule 41 makes provision with certain modifications for the admissibility of written experts' reports without the expert being called.

Evidence by Deposition or Examination of the Court

In those exceptional circumstances, where a witness is unable to attend court through infirmity or cannot conveniently be asked to come from abroad to attend court, you should consult Order 39 for the possibility of the witness being examined locally by a judge or appointed examiner, either in this country or abroad. Whether or not this can be done abroad, will depend upon the local law. The procedure will be as at trial ie the witness may be cross-examined and re-examined: 39/8/1.

Taking your own Legal Action

31 - THE TRIAL

" THE TRIAL"

By the time you enter the court, your preparation should have enabled you to know both the facts and the appropriate law "inside out".

If neither party appears, both the claim and any counterclaim may be struck out, although they may be restored for trial: Order 35, rule 1. If only one party appears, the case may proceed to judgment, subject to it being set aside on the application of the other party, which must be made within seven days of the trial: Order 35, rule 2.

A trial may always be adjourned: Order 35, rule 3.

There may be inspection of any thing or land, wherever it may be, by the judge (and jury) provided the parties are present: Order 35, rule 8 and 35/8/2.

Judgment may be given after the death of a party: Order 35, rule 9.

The judge decides which party should begin, the order of speeches and whether to dispense with opening speeches: Order 35, rule 7.

Normally the Plaintiff starts with an opening speech, in which he outlines his claim, describes the nature of the evidence he intends to call and refers to any special points, including the relevant issues. He then calls his evidence and, whether or not the Defendant has cross-examined or put in a document, he makes his second speech. This is followed by the Defendant's case.

If the Defendant intends to call evidence, he may make an opening speech and a second speech after he has called his evidence; this in turn is followed by the Plaintiff's final speech in reply. If the Plaintiff's final speech in reply raises any fresh point or previously uncited legal authority, the Defendant has a right to comment or reply. If there are several Defendants or a third party, the judge will direct the order of speeches.

If, by virtue of the pleadings, the burden of proof has shifted to the Defendant, he will have a right to start with the result that the Plaintiff follows with his opening speech, evidence and closing speech and the Defendant makes the final speech in reply.

Assuming the judge has perused the court and trial bundles, he may well feel able to direct that there is no need for opening speeches: 35/7/1.

If the Defendant elects not to call any evidence, the Plaintiff is not entitled as a matter of right to reply to the Defendant's final speech: 35/7/1.

Not only may you use an interpreter, if necessary, but you are entitled to be assisted by a friend, known as **"McKenzie Friend"**, whether or not he be a lawyer, who may take notes and advise you on examination of your witnesses, cross-examination and what to say in your speech, although he himself may not personally address the court: **McKenzie v McKenzie (1970) 3 All ER 1034**.

32 - DRAWING UP ORDERS AND JUDGMENTS

For drawing up orders of the Master or the Judge in Chambers see under 24 **APPLICATIONS**.

If you win your case, you will have "obtained judgment", the order for which must be drawn up to enable enforcement. The wording, although simple and easy to follow, will vary according to whether you obtained judgment by default (of notice of intention to defend or service of defence), summarily or by trial. Prescribed forms of judgment are set out in Forms 39-51 of Appendix A, which are printed at the beginning of Volume 2 of the White Book.

If you were claiming a specific sum, you should have claimed interest from the time when the debt or sum became payable until the date of issue of the writ; this can obviously be calculated and claimed in the prayer. You will also be entitled to interest from the date of issue until judgment and then again from judgment until payment. The current rate of interest is 8%.

This type of interest, is of course separate from any interest that forms the subject matter of your claim. For example, you may have lent somebody £10,000 at 20% per annum for 5 years. If the debt was not intended to be repaid beforehand, you would be entitled to add 20% in accordance with the terms of your agreement. Interest on your judgment debt at 8% is **additional** to the sum due when you became entitled to make your claim.

"APPEALS"

33 - APPEALS

This book only deals with (a) appeals from the Master to the Judge in Chambers, (b) appeals from the Judge in Chambers to the Court of Appeal and (c) appeals from the Judge (after trial) to the Court of Appeal.

(a)   Appeals to Judge in Chambers

An appeal from an order or decision of a Master lies to the Judge in Chambers: Order 58, rule 1.

Your notice of appeal (for which see PF 110 Vol 2 of the White Book) must be issued within five days from the hearing before the Master and served on the other party within a further five days: Order 58, rule 1(3).

The mere issuing and serving of a notice of appeal does not of itself operate to stay the proceedings or order of the Master; therefore an application for a stay might have to be made.

The party, who has appealed, may submit further evidence by affidavit, which was not before the Master, to the judge. The judge has a complete discretion, although he may simply endorse the Master's decision and adopt his reasoning. You may limit your appeal to the Master's order for costs: 58/1/2.

There is no need for a cross-appeal. Thus, were you to apply for summary judgment under Order 14 and the Master to give the Defendant leave to defend **on condition** that he pays a sum into court, if the Defendant were then to appeal against the condition, the judge could in fact not only dismiss the Defendant's appeal but give you summary judgment (because he has a complete discretion): 58/1/2.

In view of the time limits, it is not necessary for you to have the Master's order drawn up before appealing against it: 51/1/3.

You may apply to the Master for an extension of the time for appeal and, after the time has expired, you may apply to the judge for an extension of time: 58/1/5.

Appeals from Masters are initially placed in a general list but will be transferred to the Chambers Appeals List or Special Appointments List without attendance provided one or all parties consider that the hearing will take longer than 30 minutes. You should endeavour to give or agree an estimate for the time of the hearing.

Taking your own Legal Action

The practice on appeals is to lodge an indexed page numbered bundle of documents, comprising your notice of appeal, the pleadings, copies of affidavits and exhibits and any relevant order; unless it be a simple case, a skeleton argument ie an outline of the points you wish to make and any legal authorities to be relied upon, and a chronology should also be included in the bundle. If the date has been fixed, you should lodge your bundle, which should, if possible, be agreed with the other party, at least three days before the date of any hearing, which has been fixed, or within 48 hours after you have been notified that the appeal is in the list warned for hearing. In this latter case, the skeleton argument and chronology may be lodged only 24 hours before the hearing. If you wish to put in fresh documents (that were not before the Master), they should be included in the bundle and you should lodge any original affidavit with **copies** of the exhibits. Documents are to be lodged in Room W15.

Similar provisions apply to appeals to the Judge in Chambers outside London: 58/1/7 and likewise to appeals from a District Judge: 58/1/8.

In the case of appeals from District Judges, the time limits of five days and two days, referred to under rule 1(3) above, are seven days and three days respectively: Order 58, rule 2(2).

Exceptionally, where the Master has, with the written consent of the parties, heard what would otherwise be the trial: Order 36, rule 11 or assessed damages or the value of goods: Order 37 or assessed interest: Order 58, rule 2(1)(b), the appeal is to the Court of Appeal: Order 58, rule 2(1). As you need leave, ask the Master; if he refuses, you will have to seek leave to appeal from the Court of Appeal itself.

(b)   Appeal from Judge in Chambers to Court of Appeal

Should you wish to appeal from the order or decision of the **Judge in Chambers**, the appeal will be to the Court of Appeal: Order

58, rule 6. You will invariably require leave from the judge or the Court of Appeal itself and should consult Order 59 and the notes thereto, which are lengthy. A prescribed form of notice of appeal to the Court of Appeal is set out at Note 59/3/9.

Basically there are two types of appeal, "interlocutory" and "final", which are mutually exclusive. If the decision appealed from was "final", no leave is required but if it was "interlocutory" you require leave from the judge or Court of Appeal. For example, in a personal injuries case, where the questions of liability and assessment of damages are split ie tried separately, both decisions are "final". On the other hand, orders for summary judgment or striking out of the claim are not "final" but "interlocutory" because, had the Defendant been given leave to defend or the claim not struck out, the action would have continued. Apart from having to seek leave, interlocutory appeals are (placed in a different list and) generally heard and decided by two not three Court of Appeal judges.

If leave to appeal is required, it must be obtained before service of the notice of appeal: 59/1/51. The same applies, if the Respondent wishes to cross-appeal: 59/1/52.

Fresh evidence may be submitted on an appeal from the Judge in Chambers to the Court of Appeal: 59/10/11, subject to leave, which is sought by a summons heard by the Registrar to the Court of Appeal: 59/10/14. The main consideration will be why the evidence was not put before the Master and Judge in Chambers.

(c) Appeals to the Court of Appeal

As in all other proceedings, there is invariably a provision in the judge's order for liberty to apply. This would be used for the purpose of clarifying, varying or implementing the judge's order and should be distinguished from an appeal proper: 59/1/3.

Taking your own Legal Action

Although there are many exceptions, where leave is required: see table at 59/1/28, you are unlikely to be concerned with them. Basically, if you lose, you have a **right** of appeal against the judge's decision on both law and fact, including the amount of damages ordered.

As appeals are against actual decisions, you cannot appeal against an order or decision that was given in your favour simply because you disagree with the judge's reasoning or reasons: 59/1/6 (but see below).

Exceptionally, there are **circumstances preventing an appeal**, the two most likely of which to concern you would be where (i) there was an agreement between the parties not to appeal from the judge and (ii) the amount at stake is trifling: 59/1/25. Note also that the Court of Appeal may order security for costs: 59/10/19.

What you have to consider is whether the judge took a mistaken view of the facts derived from the evidence, drew the wrong inferences, wrongly exercised a discretion and/or misdirected himself as to the law.

For its part, the Court of Appeal, whilst giving due weight to the judge's views and especially to the fact that the judge was in a better position to assess the demeanour of witnesses, must "rehear" the case: this does not mean that the witnesses are called again but that the Court of Appeal looks at the transcript of the evidence and judgment and the judge's notes, when hearing argument. It is more likely to disagree with the inferences drawn by the judge than to reject his initial findings of fact: 59/1/55.

With regard to an appeal against quantum of damages, the principle is that the Court of Appeal will not vary the amount simply if it disagrees with it but only if it was wildly too high or too low: 59/10/16.

The Court of Appeal will rarely reverse the discretion of a judge, who has given reasons for its exercise, unless he misunderstood the facts or made a mistake of law: 59/1/56.

The **general powers of the Court of Appeal** are very wide and are set out in Order 59, rule 10 and the notes thereto, and include the arguing of a **point not made before the trial judge**: 59/10/6.

Fresh evidence may be admitted provided (a) you were unable, having made a proper effort, to obtain the evidence, (b) its nature is important if not crucial and (c) it is credible: 59/10/9.

The Court of Appeal is bound by its own **previous decisions** and the House of Lords. In theory, **there is only one Court of Appeal**. As, however, the Court of Appeal comprises the Master of the Rolls and thirty-five Lords Justices of Appeal, who could theoretically sit simultaneously in over ten separate courts, each including three judges, it is possible for one "court" not to be aware of a decision of one of the other "courts". Thus exceptionally the Court of Appeal will decide a point afresh, (a) if there are two of its own previous decisions, which conflict with each other, (b) where its previous decision was inconsistent with a House of Lords decision or (c) where its previous decision was *per incuriam* in that it overlooked a statute or other binding case.

The Court of Appeal has power to order a **new trial**: Order 59. rule 11.

As in the case of the trial itself, the **Court of Appeal should not be informed of** there being a **payment into court** until they have delivered judgment, unless it is relevant to the judge's order for costs: Order 59, rule 12A.

Order 59, rule 14 deals with **applications** (as opposed to appeals) to the Court of Appeal. Unless made ex parte, these are made by summons in the usual way and may be heard by the Registrar, a single Lord Justice or, "on appeal", by two Lords Justices.

Briefly, if you wish to appeal, you must serve your **Notice of Appeal** within four weeks of the judgment or order or within seven days of leave to appeal being granted: Order 59, rule 4. Your notice of appeal, whether against the whole or merely part of the judge's order, should set out your **grounds of appeal** and state the order that you believe the judge should have made: Order 59, rule 3(2). Your notice of appeal does not have to be issued or sealed but only served on the Respondent to the appeal: 59/3/3.

In your Notice of Appeal you should refer to any relevant evidence and indicate why the judge's findings should be reversed; for example, because they are inconsistent or he failed to appreciate the significance of facts accepted by him: 59/3/6.

Then you must pay the fee and lodge the necessary documents within seven days of service: 59/1/4. This means that if you serve by first class post, you should serve it on or before two days before the last day: 59/4/3. Thereafter seek the guidance of the court staff as to listing and further requirements.

The time for appealing can be abridged, if it is urgent, or extended, in which case the court considers the length of the delay, the reasons for it, the prospect of success and whether the Respondent will have been prejudiced; the Respondent is allowed to consent to an extension of time for appeal: 59/4/4.

If you are the Respondent to the appeal and fully agree with the decision of the judge, you need do nothing save prepare for the appeal. If, however, you wish to argue that (a) the judge's decision should be varied, if the appeal is wholly or partially allowed, (b) the judge was right but for "the wrong reasons", ie he should have decided in your favour on different grounds, or (c) the judge was wholly or partly wrong: Order 59, rule 6(1) you must within 21 days serve a **"Respondent's Notice"**: Order 59, rule 6(3) and (as in the case of the appellant) pay the fee and lodge two copies with the court office: Order 59, rule 6(4). See also 59/6/1, which refers to a Respondent's Notice to Affirm, a Respondent's Notice to Vary and a Respondent's Notice by way of Cross-appeal.

Both a Notice of Appeal and a Respondent's Notice may be **amended** at any time by leave or before the appeal is entered in "the list of forthcoming appeals": Order 59, rule 7. Once again, the amendment, called a "**Supplementary Notice**" must be served and two copies of it lodged with the court.

Setting down your appeal merely entails lodging a copy of the judgment or order and two copies of your notice of appeal, one of them bearing the receipt for the fee in the Civil Appeals General Office (Room E330); thereafter the court assigns your appeal to the appropriate list: Order 59, rule 5.

After you have set down your appeal, **the court will write to you**, confirming that your appeal has been set down and informing you as to further requirements. Within four days you must notify the Respondents that your appeal has been entered and provide them with the reference number: 59/5/10.

As a litigant in person, the Civil Appeals Office will send you the "**Appeal Bundle Leaflet**" and the "**Application Bundle Leaflet**" and a "**Check List**". Furthermore, **skeleton arguments** are optional for litigants in person.

In most cases the Court of Appeal will require **transcripts** of the judgment and relevant evidence. You should start to obtain these as soon as possible, as they will, along with other documents, be required for the appeal bundles, which should be lodged within 14 days of the appeal being listed: Order 59, rule 9.

The transcripts to be lodged must be **official originals** and not copies: 59/9/5 unless the evidence or judgment were not recorded by shorthand or tape: 59/9/6, in which case the **judge's notes** of the evidence or judgment will have to suffice. If the judge took no note, the parties must endeavour to agree their own notes and submit them to the judge for his approval. This and other matters, including skeleton arguments are covered by a Practice Statement, which is set out at 59/17A and 17B.

Appeals cannot usually be withdrawn without leave; generally they are **dismissed "by consent"**. Appeals may however be **allowed by**

consent but this would be rare because it would effectively mean that the Court of Appeal is endorsing the parties' opinion that the judge's decision was wrong: 59/1/21.

Finally, you may appeal from the Court of Appeal to the **House of Lords** subject to obtaining leave from the Court of Appeal, which it would be sensible to do at the end of the hearing of the appeal, (or from the House of Lords itself). For appeals to the House of Lords see Volume 2 Part 16 of the White Book.

34 - COSTS

There are two types of costs. First, **"Standard costs"**, which are all those costs reasonably incurred. If there is any doubt as to what is reasonable, it must be resolved in favour of the **paying party** (ie the one ordered to pay the costs) rather than the **receiving party** (ie the one, in whose favour the order for costs has been made): Order 62, rule 12. Secondly there are **"Indemnity costs"**, which are far more generous to the receiving party; any doubt as to whether such costs were reasonable is to be resolved in favour of the receiving party: Order 62, rule 12. Unless the court states otherwise, standard costs apply: Order 62, rule 12(3).

The fundamental rule is that the award of costs is within the discretion of the court. That discretion, however, must be exercised in accordance with well-established principles and be ordered by the court (ie Master or Judge) and not left to the Taxing Officer, who is the "judge" for the purposes of assessing the **amount** of the costs. Usually **costs follow the event**, which means that the successful party should be awarded his costs.

Therefore it is essential to remember at the end of each hearing you "win" (even if it be only an adjournment) to ask the Master or judge for your costs. It is also important to understand the main types of order, which can be made.

"Costs" and **"Costs in any event"**, if ordered in your favour, mean that your costs have to be paid regardless of the eventual outcome of the case. This type of order is made, where the court considers that you have been fully justified in making your application whatever the eventual outcome of the case.

"Plaintiff's costs in the cause" means that you will receive your costs in respect of that part of the case, if you ultimately win the case but **not have to pay them** if you ultimately lose the case; similarly with **"Defendant's costs in the cause"**. These types of orders are a half way house between "costs in any event" and "costs in the cause" and are generally awarded, where the court feels that **on balance** you should have that particular benefit or concession.

"Costs in the cause" are costs ordered during interlocutory proceedings and will be awarded to the party, who eventually wins the case. Similarly, **"Costs in application"** will be awarded to the party, who eventually wins the application.

"Costs reserved" means that the question of who should pay and receive them is postponed and invariably results in an order in favour of the party who ultimately wins the application or trial.

"No order as to costs" means that the court feels that neither party really deserves any costs eg it was "six of one and half a dozen of the other"!

Occasionally the court omits to make any order as to costs, in which case it is arguable as to whether or not they can be obtained because current practice differs.

"Costs thrown away" are usually awarded to a party, who has been obliged to do something that he might not otherwise have had to do. For example, if you amend without leave, you will have to pay the "costs thrown away", which have been caused by your amendment: Order 62, rule 6(5), eg the costs of any Amended Defence that has to be drafted and served.

Taking your own Legal Action

Where a **party discontinues**, the other party will be deemed to be entitled to his costs: Order 62, rule 5(3).

If you accept a **payment into court**, there is deemed to have been made an order for costs in your favour in respect of everything that you have had to do up to the time, at which you give notice of your acceptance: Order 62, rule 5(4).

Similarly if you apply for an extension of time, you will have to pay the costs in any event: Order 62, rule 6(6). If served with a notice to admit under Order 27, you may well have to pay the costs in respect of the proof of those facts, which you failed to admit: Order 62, rule 6(7).

The court may "assess" the costs and order such gross sum to be paid, thereby obviating the need for the costs to be taxed; it is unlikely to do this unless specifically so requested or in minor County Court applications: Order 62, rule 7(4). The **court may** also **apportion** the costs, if it would be fair to do so.

Unless the court specifically orders **"taxation forthwith"**, the taxation of costs is always left until after the conclusion of the case: Order 62, rule 8.

As a litigant in person, you are entitled to be reimbursed for any reasonable disbursements in full and costs reasonably incurred in obtaining legal advice.If you can prove that you have suffered pecuniary loss ie by having had to miss work, you may obtain up to two-thirds of what you would have been charged by a solicitor; if not, you will be limited to being able to charge at the rate of £9.25 an hour: Order 62, rule 18(3). If you are allowed your costs for attending court to conduct your own case, you will not in addition be entitled to a witness allowance for yourself.

To maximise your claim for costs, it is eminently sensible to obtain the services of a recognised costs draftsman, which many solicitors, who do not employ their own in-house costs draftsmen, do. Costs draftsmen are specialists and will charge you 5%-7% of the amount of the costs claimed. They may also be permitted with the court's leave to assist you as **a Mackenzie Friend** at the hearing for the taxation of costs.

Should you have had the misfortune to have been represented by a solicitor, whose bill of costs you regard as too high, you have the right under Section 70 of the Solicitors Act 1974 to challenge his bill of costs and have it taxed provided you issue an originating summons in the Supreme Court Taxing Office within one calendar month of the bill having been delivered.Thereafter the court has a discretion to order the bill of costs to be taxed. In three specific instances no order will be made, unless you can establish special circumstances: see White Book Volume 2 Section 70(3) of the Solicitors Act 1974 and the note thereto.

Should you choose to consult the White Book, you will observe that Order 62 is one of the longest orders: do not, however, be daunted, since, after a cursory perusal, you will see that very few rules and notes are likely to be relevant.

The **procedure for taxations** is laid down in Part V of Order 62 in rules 29-32. If you are dissatisfied with the decision of the taxing officer, (a District Judge in the County Court) you may ask him to **review** his own decision: rules 33 and 34 and, if you are still dissatisfied, you may ask a judge to review the taxation: rule 35.

YOU THE PLAINTIFF IN THE COUNTY COURT
References are to the County Court Rules 1981 ("CCR")

35 - WITNESSES

As the same principles apply as in the High Court, see Section 1.

Taking your own Legal Action

36 - SETTLING YOUR CASE

As the same principles apply as in the High Court, see Section 2.

37 - STARTING PROCEEDINGS

In the County Court, an action is started by a **"Plaint"**: CCR Order 3, rule 1. The Plaint is the County Court equivalent of the Writ in the High Court. There are basically two types of action: a **"fixed date action"**, which is for money/damages only: Order 3, rule 2(1) and a **"default action"**, which is for any other type of remedy: Order 3, rule 2(2). In either case, there is prescribed form, which you should obtain from any County Court.

Issue

To start the action you have to request the court to issue a Summons for either a default or a fixed date action (alternatively you may yourself fill out the appropriate Summons form: Order 3, rule 3(1A)), lodge the form with as many copies of the Particulars of Claim as there are Defendants plus one for the court and pay the appropriate fee.

Venue

You may start your action in the court (a) where the Defendant or one of them lives or carries on business, (b) the district where the cause of action arose or (c) if it is a default action, in any County Court: Order 4, rule 2.

You should, however, consider what might well turn out to be a more appropriate course of action. For example, if the Defendant puts in a Defence, the court will transfer the case to his "home" court, which of course may be extremely inconvenient for you, if he lives far away. In addition, if there was an accident or if the Defendant and all the witnesses live away from you, the County Court for that area might be more appropriate. You should therefore carefully consider the venue at the outset, as a transfer will only result in delay.

Fees

The fees to issue are from £10 to £500, depending on the value of your claim. The fee for applications (which were free) are £20 for a District Judge, £30 for a Judge but only £10 for an ex parte application or a consent order. If your claim is non-monetary, eg for an injunction **only**, the fee is £80.

Service

Unlike the High Court (where the Plaintiff serves the Defendant), the County Court itself will serve the Defendant with the summons by sending it to him by first class post: CCR Order 7, rule 10(1)(b), unless you choose personally to **deliver** it to the Defendant: Order 7, rule 10(1)(a), or the Defendant's solicitor agrees, by giving a certificate, that he will accept service on behalf of the Defendant: Order 7, rule 11. Fourthly, if the summons has been returned by the Post Office "undelivered" or "gone away", it can be served by the bailiff: Order 7, rule 10(4).

In any event, good service on the Defendant will be deemed to have taken place,if he defends or admits the claim or makes a counterclaim: Order 7, rule 12.

A partnership is served by delivery to a **partner personally** or by post to the **firm's address**: Order 7, rule 13. If the partnership is

Taking your own Legal Action

known to have been dissolved, you should ensure that you or the court serves each of the partners you are suing: Order 7, rule 13(2).

With regard to a body corporate eg a local authority, service may be effected on the Mayor or Chief Executive etc: Order 7, rule 14(1).

Although a registered company may be served at any **relevant** place of business: Order 7, rule 14(2), it is advisable to serve its registered office to avoid a default judgment being too readily set aside: Order 7, rule 14(3).

In any event, the court should send you a "notice of service", in which it will indicate when the Defendant has been **deemed** to have been served, from which you will be able to calculate if and when you may enter **default judgment**. If it is a default action for a specific sum, the court will have included a Request for Default Judgment form, which you may use. If, however, your claim is for general damages, you may still apply for judgment but, as your damages will have to be assessed, you should ask for an order for **interlocutory judgment** with an appointment for the assessment of damages and costs: Order 9, rule 6, and give a time estimate.

Parties

You may sue a Defendant for more than one cause of action, if he is liable in the same capacity: Order 5, rule 1. You may sue jointly with another or sue two or more Defendants, if your claims all arose from the same transaction: Order 5, rule 2 but equally the court has power to order separate trials: Order 5, rule 3.

38 - PARTICULARS OF CLAIM

Just as a Writ must be accompanied by a Statement of Claim, so - in the County Court - must the Plaint be accompanied by the

Particulars of Claim, the contents and principles for the pleading of which are identical. In other words, whatever your cause of action, the same form of wording in the body of the pleading should be used. You should briefly state the material facts: CCR Order 6, rule 1(1).

If you are claiming general damages and do not include in the prayer to your claim "damages limited to £5,000", this will automatically confer jurisdiction on the District Judge (as opposed to the Judge) to hear your claim: CCR Order 21, rule 5(1); the District Judge can hear claims for any value with the parties' consent.

If they are extremely short, you will be able and may include your Particulars of Claim in the space provided in the (Request for issue of) Summons: Order 6, rule 1(2). Otherwise they should be filed separately: Order 6, rule 1(4).

If you are claiming any of the following, you should plead them in both the Particulars and the Prayer:-interest: Order 6, rule 1A, aggravated exemplary or provisional damages: Order 6, rule 1B, an account: Order 6, rule 2. If you are claiming an injunction or declaration over land, it should be identified: Order 6, rule 4. There are special requirements for HP claims: see Order 6, rule 6.

In personal injury cases, unless you file a medical report and schedule of special damages with your Particulars of Claim: Order 6, rule 1(5), the court may extend your time to do so, dispense with the requirement, if you are not intending to rely on a medical report or have no special damages, or stay the proceedings, which means prevent you from carrying on: Order 6, rule 1(6).

The **heading** will be different: instead of "In the High Court of Justice" "Queens Bench Division", it will say "In the Newchester County Court"; the **title** of the parties will be the same; instead of "Statement of Claim" it will say "Particulars of Claim"; and after the Prayer (see Section 6 and Form 5) instead of stating "Served etc" it will say "Dated this   day of   1997" and finally be addressed "To the Defendant and the District Judge".

Taking your own Legal Action

39 - JUDGMENT IN DEFAULT

Default Action

The Defendant has 14 days from service, in which to admit liability wholly or partly (and seek time for payment), defend and/or counterclaim: Order 9, rule 2(1), which he should do by filing the relevant document/pleading with the court: rule 2(6), whereupon the court should send you a copy: rule 2(7) and notify you of a date for the pre-trial review (PTR) or trial: rule 5. If the Defendant fails to do this, on the fifteenth day you may enter judgment by so requesting in writing: rule 6. As there is always a delay by the court in dealing with matters, it is sensible to telephone on the fifteenth day to see what, if anything, the Defendant has done, and, if nothing, fax, deliver or send your Request for Default Judgment, using the form provided by the court and stating if you have been paid anything: rule 6(1). If your claim is for unliquidated ie general damages, you should request interlocutory judgment and an appointment for damages to be assessed and costs: rule 6(2). You will be entitled to interest, whether on the whole sum under rule 6(1) or under rule 3 (where you accept a lesser sum admitted by the Defendant): rule 8.

If the Defendant files his admission, Defence or Counterclaim late but before you have entered judgment, it is valid: rule 9.

If a Defence is filed in an action for a liquidated ie specific sum, the case is usually transferred to the Defendant's "home court" ie the county court for the area where he lives: rule 2(8). Rule 3 deals with admissions and requests for time to pay.

Fixed Date Action

Although the Defendant should file the relevant admission/Defence (and Counterclaim) within 14 days under rule 2, you may only apply for **judgment** to the extent that the Defendant has admitted liability: rule 4 or for judgment or directions, where the action is not only a fixed date action but also one where the automatic directions under Order 17, rule 11 apply: rule 4A. Even without filing and delivering a Defence, the Defendant may defend on the day, although he is likely to have to pay the costs: rule 9(3).

40 - DIRECTIONS

Directions may be made at the pre-trial review: Order 3, rule 3(3), on the hearing of applications: Order 13 (see also Section 55 **APPLICATIONS**) or automatically under Order 17, rule 11. Note, by looking at Order 17, rule 11(1), that the automatic directions do not apply to some 17 types of action.

As, however, the automatic directions are likely to apply in most cases: see Order 17, rule 11(3)-(8), it is worth briefly referring to them.

Automatic Directions

When pleadings are deemed to be closed, which is 14 days after delivery of Defence or 28 days after delivery of Counterclaim, discovery should be made within 28 days and inspection within a further 7 days. Unless otherwise ordered, you should endeavour to exchange and agree the written reports of experts, photographs, sketch plans and police accident reports and simultaneously exchange witness statements. The normal period for this is 10 weeks from close of pleadings. If the experts' reports are not agreed, you may call up to 2 experts to give oral evidence. In a personal injuries case, you may have 2 medical experts and one other expert: rule 11(7).

As Plaintiff, you should ask the court to fix a hearing date within 6 months. **If you do not do so within 15 months from the day pleadings are closed, your action will be AUTOMATICALLY**

Taking your own Legal Action

STRUCK OUT. You would, however, be able to **start** all over **again**, **provided** you are within the limitation period.

Pre-trial Review

The PTR: see Order 17, rule 1 corresponds with the High Court's summons for directions under RSC Order 25. The two orders, however, are not identical, because there would appear to be no duty on the **parties** to give all appropriate information to the District Judge (as set out in RSC Order 25, rule 6).

The District Judge has to try to limit the issues by securing admissions and agreements: rule 2, corresponding with RSC Order 24, rule 4, although there seem to be no adverse costs implications involved. Similarly the parties should notify each other of and apply for any directions they consider relevant, although again there is no reference to costs: rule 3, corresponding with RSC Order 25, rule 7.

If you do not appear, your action may be struck out or directions given: Order 17, rule 5. The District Judge may give judgment (a) if the Defendant admits the claim, (b) if the Defendant has neither appeared nor delivered a Defence or (c) subject to proof by you, where there is a Defence but no Defendant: Order 17, rules 6-8.

Unlike the High Court, the County Court fixes the trial date after the PTR: Order 17, rule 9. It can also fix a PTR on its own initiative: Order 17, rule 10.

41 - AUTOMATIC STRIKING OUT

If you do nothing for 12 months after service - even if there has been an admission - your action will be struck out and will not be reinstated: Order 9, rule 10.

Your action will also be struck out automatically under Order 17, rule 11(9): see Section 40 **DIRECTIONS** above.

42 - SUMMARY JUDGMENT

As in the High Court you may apply for summary judgment: Order 9, rule 14 with an affidavit in support served on the Defendant not less than seven days before the hearing: Order 9, rule 14(3) on the ground that the Defendant has no Defence, even though he has delivered a document titled "Defence": Order 9, rule 14(1A).

Such an application may be heard on a PTR and is subject to the same practice as in the High Court: RSC Order 14 but is not available for arbitrations: Order 9, rule 14(1)(a).

It should be distinguished from an application to strike out under Order 13, rule 5(1)(a) where you argue that there is no reasonable Defence as a matter of law: this last application does not need any affidavit in support.

43 - DELAY

As the same principles apply as in the High Court: see Section 10. In addition, delays are caused by the County Court, whose staff are continuing to struggle with a backlog of correspondence.

44 - CORRESPONDENCE

See Section 11.

45 - ON RECEIPT OF DEFENCE

As the same principles apply as in the High Court, see Section 12.

46 - FURTHER PLEADINGS

A **"Reply"** is not mentioned in the CCR and therefore theoretically does not exist. If the Defendant files a counterclaim, the court will notify you of a PTR. If, however, you receive a counterclaim, there is no reason why you should not proceed to file and deliver a (Reply and) Defence to Counterclaim, for which the practice is the same as in the High Court: see Section 13, thereby getting on with the case and leaving less to be dealt with by way of directions.

47 - FURTHER PARTICULARS

For some strange reason,Further and Better Particulars are correctly called "Further Particulars" in the County Court.

Further Particulars of the Particulars of Claim may be ordered on application or by the court: Order 6, rule 7(1) and, if necessary, before filing a Defence: Order 6, rule 7(2). The application may be refused, if made without prior request: Order 6, rule 7(3). Further Particulars should be filed and supplied in one document: Order 6, rule 7(4), in which each Request is followed by the appropriate answer.

For obtaining Further Particulars of the Defence: see Order 9, rule 11, which is similar to Order 6, rule 7. The High Court practice is helpful: see RSC Order 18, rule 12 and note 18/12/1.

48 - AMENDMENTS

Amendments are dealt with by Order 15, which roughly corresponds with RSC Order 20: see Section 15. Pleadings may be amended or parties added, struck out or substituted as in the High Court: Order 15, rule 1.

Whereas in the High Court pleadings may be amended once without leave before pleadings are deemed to be closed: RSC Order 20, rule 3, in the County Court they may be amended more than once without leave before the return day ie the PTR: Order 15, rule 2. Obviously, if you amend your claim, the Defendant's time for defence is extended by a further 14 days.

49 - ORGANIZATION

See Section 16.

50 - INTERIM PAYMENTS

As Order 13, rule 12(1) incorporates the provisions of RSC Order 29, Part II, see Section 17. The only material difference is that you must serve your affidavit in support seven not ten days before the application: Order 13, rule 12(2).

51 - DISCOVERY

As the same principles apply as in the High Court, see Section 18. In the County Court, discovery is dealt with by Order 14, rules 1-10 and Order 17, rule 11(5) and (6).

In an action for personal injuries arising from a road accident, discovery is limited to documents relating to damages: Order 17, rule 11(5)(c).

52 - INSPECTION

As the same principles apply as in the High Court, see Section 19. In the County Court inspection is dealt with by Order 14, rules 3-10 and by Order 17, rule 11(5)(d).

53 - INTERROGATORIES

As Order 14, rule 11 incorporates the provisions of RSC Order 26, see Section 22. The only material difference is that where you choose to administer interrogatories without order you have to include a **notice** of the other party's right to have the interrogatories varied or withdrawn: Order 14, rule 11(1A).

54 - PAYMENTS INTO COURT

As the same principles apply as in the High Court, see Section 21. In the County Court payments into court are dealt with by Order 11.

55 - APPLICATIONS

These are dealt with by Order 13, rule 1 of which mirrors the High Court practice. Consequently see Section 24, remembering to substitute "Application" for "Summons", "District Judge" for "Master" and "Judge" for "Judge in Chambers".

Where a party applies to the court before a PTR has been fixed, the court may, on the hearing of the application treat the hearing as a PTR (the County Court equivalent of a Summons for Directions) and give directions in accordance with Order 17: Order 13, rule 2(4).

56 - FIXING HEARINGS

Unless a day for the hearing has already been fixed by the court, the Plaintiff should apply to the court for a date, giving an agreed, if possible, estimate of the time necessary and stating the number of witnesses to be called: Order 17, rule 11(8).

Thereafter the Defendant should tell the Plaintiff 14 days before the hearing which documents he wishes to put before the court so that the Plaintiff can prepare an agreed paginated and indexed bundle, which he should send to the court seven days before the hearing: Order 17, rule 12(2) and (3). He should also send two copies of any Further Particulars and Interrogatories with their answers and of all the witness statements and experts' reports that have been exchanged, indicating such matters or parts of statements or reports that have been agreed: Order 17, rule 12(3). (Thus the procedure is far simpler than in the High Court).

57 - INJUNCTIONS

As the same principles apply as in the High Court, see Section 27. In the County Court injunctions and other similar types of order are covered by Order 13, rules 6 and 7.

58 - EVIDENCE

As the same principles apply as in the High Court, see Section 30. In the County Court the rules are set out in Order 20 *Part II - Evidence generally* (rules 4-11), *Part III - Summoning and examination of witnesses* (rules 12 and 13), *Part IV - Hearsay evidence* (rules 14-26) and *Part V - Expert evidence* (rules 27 and 28).

59 - THE TRIAL

As the same principles apply as in the High Court, see Section 31. In the County Court Order 21 deals with non-appearance by the Plaintiff: rule 1, failure by the Plaintiff to prove his claim: rule 2, non-appearance or admission by the Defendant: rule 3 and counterclaims:

rule 4. If between the date of notification and the hearing, you receive any payment, you must notify the other side: rule 3A.

You should also note that by rule 5(1) the **District Judge** may hear the action if (a) the Defendant fails to appear or admits the claim, (b) the parties consent or (c) **the value of your claim is not more than £5,000.**

Finally, the judge may decide who has the right to begin, the order and number of speeches and whether to dispense with an opening speech: rule 5A. There is also power to inspect a place or thing: rule 6.

60 - DRAWING UP OF JUDGMENTS AND ORDERS

Unlike the High Court, in the County Court all orders and judgments are drawn up by the court. It is, however, prudent to make a note at the time, especially as the order is rarely posted for several days and applies from the moment it is pronounced.

61 - APPEALS

The County Court rules do not themselves deal with appeals from the Judge (or District Judge) to the Court of Appeal, although the right to appeal is conferred by Section 77 of the County Courts Act 1984.

You will need leave to appeal either from the Judge or from the Court of Appeal where the value of your appeal, which means the amount awarded, has not exceeded £5,000 or where the Judge was acting in an appellate capacity (ie your case had originally been heard by the District Judge before you appealed to the Judge). If, however, the Judge dismisses the claim, the "value" element, is the amount of the claim. Thus, if you were either claiming more than £5,000 or **reasonably expecting** to obtain more than £5,000, say in a personal injuries case, you would **not** need leave to appeal. For further detail consult RSC Order 59, rule 19 and notes 59/19/1-13 and 59/1/34 in the White Book.

62 - COSTS

As the same principles apply as in the High Court, see Section 34.

In the County Court costs are dealt with under Order 38, rule 17 of which deals specifically with litigants in person.

If the costs have been taxed and a party is dissatisfied with the decision of the District Judge on any item, you may request the District Judge to **reconsider** his decision: Order 38, rule 24(1). If you are still dissatisfied after a reconsideration, you may "appeal" to the Judge to **review** the taxation: Order 38, rule 24(4).

IN THE SMALL CLAIMS COURT

63 - ARBITRATION

This should be distinguished from arbitration under the Arbitration Acts and is really another way of describing small claims and how they are dealt with.

Whereas the procedure in the High Court and County Court is similar, if not identical, there are radical differences in arbitrations, the whole procedure being very much simpler.

Jurisdiction

Apart from asking for arbitration (when you start the proceedings) or all parties agreeing to it, the County Court will **automatically** refer the claim to arbitration if it is for (a) not more than

Taking your own Legal Action

£3,000 or (b) not more than £3,000, including a claim for damages for personal injuries limited to £1,000. If your claim is for more than £3,000 or, though less than £3,000, it includes a claim for more than £1,000 for damages for personal injuries, it should **not automatically** be referred to arbitration.

Practice and Procedure

This is to be found **mainly** under Order 19. The arbitrator is usually the District Judge, although the case may be referred to the Judge or "an outside arbitrator": rule 5.

Subject to his power to order the case to be tried under the full panoply of the County Court rules, the arbitrator or court itself will probably give simple directions as to the parties copying their documents for each other, exchanging experts' reports and listing witnesses: rule 6(3). There may, however, be a preliminary appointment, if it be considered that special directions are necessary or that there is no reasonable cause of action or Defence but the arbitrator should endeavour to keep the number of court hearings to a minimum: rule 6(4).

Subject to the above, the important differences are that there may be no applications for Further Particulars of either the claim or the Defence, no notices to admit facts or documents, no requirement to exchange witness statements, no facilities for making payments into court or obtaining security for costs and none of the detailed rules relating to discovery and interrogatories: rule 6(8).

Summary

Thus a small claim basically consists of the ordinary pleadings, the exchange of documents and experts' reports and the hearing itself.

The Hearing

"The hearing shall be informal and the strict rules of evidence shall not apply; unless the arbitrator orders otherwise, the hearing shall be held in private and evidence shall not be taken on oath": rule 7(3).

Provided he is fair and gives the parties a proper opportunity to put forward their case, the arbitrator may use any method of procedure or order of presenting evidence or making speeches or submissions and will doubtless assist parties by explaining any legal terms and putting his own questions to witnesses and the parties in order to assist them and arrive at a just decision: rule 7(4). Having made his award, he should, like all judges, give reasons: rule 7(8).

64 - COSTS

In theory the arbitrator may award costs: Order 19, rule 10 but in practice the only costs that you may obtain are the court issue fee, the cost of reimbursing witnesses' travelling expenses, not more than £29 for your own or your witnesses' loss of earnings and not more than £112.50 by way of expert witness's fee: Order 19, rule 4.

There is, however, one important exception, namely that the arbitrator may direct that costs be paid "where there has been unreasonable conduct on the part of the opposite party": rule 4(2)(c), in which case they will not be taxed but assessed at the time: rule 4(5).

65 - SETTING ASIDE AN ARBITRATION

In theory you cannot appeal from the arbitrator. In practice, however, you can, although it is called "a setting aside" and is limited to where the arbitrator has misconducted himself or, more likely, made

an error of law: Order 19, rule 8. An application to set aside will be made to the Judge and in practice treated like any other appeal from the District Judge.

PART 3 - YOU THE DEFENDANT IN THE HIGH COURT

66 - GENERAL

See Part 2, Sections 1-34 and below.

67 - ACKNOWLEDGMENT OF SERVICE FORM

Service of Writ (endorsed with Statement of Claim) **unaccompanied** by the prescribed form of acknowledgment of service **or** with the form but **without the title and number of the action** is irregular: RSC Order 10, rule 1(6) and 10/1/13. Unless you wish to ignore the irregularity, it should be returned to the Plaintiff with a covering letter, indicating the irregularity. The Plaintiff, however, will obviously re-serve the Writ properly but it may gain you further time.

As Defendant, you should acknowledge service by completing the form with your full name and your residential address or, if you have no address within the jurisdiction, an address, at which documents will reach you, and by signing it: Order 12, rule 3(2)(a). You should then personally lodge or post the acknowledgment in accordance with the Guidance Notes. You should do this, even if you wish merely to contest the proceedings as being irregular or without jurisdiction: 12/1/1. Proper acknowledgment by you will not waive any irregularity nor prevent you from contesting the proceedings, which you may do by applying by summons: Order 12, rule 8. The issue and service of such a summons will (a) automatically extend the time for serving a Defence and (b) prevent the Plaintiff from entering judgment in default of Defence: 12/7-8/3.

Taking your own Legal Action

68 - ACTION ON RECEIPT OF CLAIM

Having acknowledged service (also known as "entering an appearance": Order 12, rule 10) and assuming you have given notice of intention to defend, your next step will depend on when you receive the Statement of Claim. If the Writ is not endorsed with or accompanied by a Statement of Claim, you need do nothing until the Statement of Claim is served. You may, however, wish to try to settle the Plaintiff's claim, see Section 2 above. If the Writ is endorsed with or accompanied by a Statement of Claim (and has been properly served), you have 28 days from the date of service (unless the Plaintiff agrees to extend your time) to serve your Defence: Order 18, rule 2 regardless of the date on which you acknowledged service: 18/2/1. If the Statement of Claim is served more than 14 days after service of the Writ, you have a further 14 days thereafter, in which to serve your Defence. Thus you never have less than 28 days from service of the Writ for service of your Defence.

You will not have to serve your Defence, if (a) in the meantime the Plaintiff serves a summons under Order 14, which automatically extends your time, (b) you serve a summons under Order 12, rule 8 disputing the jurisdiction of the court: see 67 **ACKNOWLEDGMENT OF SERVICE** or (c) having failed to obtain an extension of time by consent, you issue and serve a time summons under Order 3, rule 5: see 24 **APPLICATIONS** *Time for service* paragraph 3.

69 - PRELIMINARY APPLICATIONS

Apart from applications under Order 12, rule 8 (disputing jurisdiction or regularity of proceedings), Order 3, rule 5 (time summons) and Order 14 (summary judgment), you may before serving your Defence apply (i) to strike out the claim: Order 18, rule 19, (ii) for discovery (even before service of the Statement of Claim): 24/3/2 and 18/12/24, (iii) for Further and Better Particulars where they would be "necessary or desirable to enable" you to plead your Defence: Order 18, rule 12(5) and 18/12/23 *(1) Time for Particulars by Order* or (iv) exceptionally for leave to administer interrogatories, provided that it is clear what will be in dispute: 26/1/21.

If soundly based, such applications, if made early on, may bring a speedy end to the Plaintiff's claim, thus saving unnecessary costs and avoiding the trauma of protracted litigation. Simply because a normal action may proceed according to the various steps that are set out in the rules, in the order in which they appear, does not mean that an appropriate application made exceptionally early would not be justified in the circumstances of the particular claim.

70 - SUMMARY JUDGMENT

If you are served with a summons under Order 14 for summary judgment, the onus is upon you to show that "there is an issue or question in dispute which ought to be tried or that there ought for some other reason to be a trial" of the claim or part of it, ie that you should be allowed to defend: Order 14, rule 3.

You may "show cause" (a) by taking a technical point on the validity of the cause of action or sufficiency of the Plaintiff's affidavit in support or (b) on the merits in that you have a good Defence or that a difficult point of law has been raised or that there is a triable issue as to the facts or the amount claimed or any other bona fide and arguable Defence. Showing cause is normally done by way of affidavit but, if you happen already to have drafted or served your Defence, this may be sufficient to defeat the Plaintiff's application, provided the Master does not consider it to be a sham: 14/3-4/3. The Defence could be exhibited to your affidavit. Your affidavit should answer the Plaintiff's affidavit in support: 14/3-4/4. A set off and Counterclaim should enable you to obtain unconditional leave to defend: 14/3-4/13. As it is not a pleading, you are advised not merely to make allegations but to set out

Taking your own Legal Action

(with or without exhibits of documents) some or all of the evidence that you would use in support of the Defence that you would wish to plead.

Admitting part of the claim will not deprive you of your right to defend the remainder of the claim. You could be ordered to make an interim payment in respect of the amount admitted or proved against you and still be allowed to defend as to the balance of the claim disputed by you.

Your affidavit should, if possible, be served not less than three days before the hearing: 14/3-4/5. The Plaintiff may put in an affidavit in reply but, if your affidavit is sufficient to show a "triable issue", he would be well advised to withdraw his summons and consent to you defending.

It is quite possible for both the Plaintiff on his claim and you on your Counterclaim: Order 14, rule 5 to obtain summary judgment against each other, in which case the smaller claim would be set off against the larger claim. On the other hand, if the Counterclaim arises from the same facts as the claim, neither party is likely to obtain summary judgment.

Another possible outcome, is that the Plaintiff obtains judgment but that it be "stayed" ie not enforced, until after the trial of the Counterclaim. If your set off or Counterclaim exceeds the claim, you will either obtain leave to defend or the claim will be stayed, whereas if it is less than the claim the Plaintiff may obtain judgment for the difference: 14/3-4/13.

Leave to defend is frequently granted on condition that a payment into court is made, usually where the Master would like to give judgment for the Plaintiff or is not convinced that the Defence is not a sham or "shadowy": 14/3-4/15. The Master may order the whole sum claimed to be paid into court as a condition for leave to defend. He should not, however, do this, if you could not afford to make the payment into court because this would mean that you were effectively deprived of the right to defend: 14/3-4/15.

71 - DEFENCE, SET OFF AND COUNTERCLAIM AND THIRD PARTY PROCEEDINGS

Defence

With regard to pleading your Defence, you are to a considerable extent constrained by the way, in which the Plaintiff has set out his allegations. Even if the Plaintiff has lumped together several distinct or alternative allegations in one paragraph, unless you wish to admit the whole paragraph, you should, preferably by separate numbered paragraphs, deal with each individual allegation, by either "not admitting" or "denying" it. If you wish, whether you have admitted, not admitted or denied the claim, to assert or put forward your own case and/or make a counterclaim, follow the **cardinal rules of pleading**: see Part 1 (d): **Drafting your Claim**.

Set off and Counterclaim

A set off is a monetary cross-claim which is also a defence to the claim made in the action: 18/17/2. It can be (a) any allegation of a fact or matter, usually a sum of money, arising from the claim itself and by which the claim is diminished or (b) such sum of money arising from a Counterclaim (which need not arise from the claim), which is equivalent to or will "eat up" the sum claimed. Thus if the value of your set off exceeds the value of the claim, the excess must be pleaded by way of Counterclaim.

A good example of a set off is a debt due from the Plaintiff to the Defendant or, in answer to a claim for the price of goods sold and delivered, a claim for damages because some of the goods ordered were (i) not delivered, (ii) not fit for their purpose, (iii) unmerchantable and/or (iv) did not accord with their description or the sample.

Taking your own Legal Action

With regard to pleading a set off, your Defence will usually end with the words "The Defendant will seek to set off [the sum of £   / so much of the sum due to him] in diminution or extinction of the Plaintiff's claim." Alternatively "the Defendant will seek to set off so much of his Counterclaim as will satisfy the Plaintiff's claim."

    With regard to pleading a Counterclaim, apart from pleading it in the Defence by way of set off, it should be fully set out, preceded by the word **"Counterclaim"** and then pleaded just as a claim would be pleaded ie with separate paragraphs for each allegation. It may well be that some of the allegations have already been pleaded in the Defence, in which case the Counterclaim should start:

"Counterclaim

21.   The Defendant repeats paragraphs 2 to 18 of the Defence."

    If you wish to counterclaim, you should do so in the same pleading as your Defence: Order 15, rule 2. Your Counterclaim need not be confined to the Plaintiff but may include another party: see 15/2/1 for comprehensive guidance as to the procedure.

Third Party Proceedings

    If you wish to sue a Third Party, you should issue your **Third Party Notice before** you serve your Defence: Order 16, rule 1(2). The procedure is complex and you should consult Order 16 generally and/or the Practice Master.

72 - APPLICATIONS

    See Sections 24, 67, 69, 70 and 73. In addition, if the Plaintiff does not pursue matters for a considerable time or fails to take out a summons for directions: Order 25, you may apply for the action to be dismissed for want of prosecution: 25/1/4. The success of such an application will depend upon you being able to prove either intentional and contumelious default or inordinate and inexcusable delay, which terms are explained and illustrated in Notes 25/1/5 to 8 of the White Book.

73 - SECURITY FOR COSTS

In principle no-one should ever be prevented from defending himself against a claim simply because he is unable to pay the potential costs of a successful Plaintiff. The corollary, however, that a Plaintiff should not be prevented from making a claim, even if he cannot pay the costs of a successful Defendant, does not apply: 23/1-3/16. Consider therefore whether you can nip the Plaintiff's claim in the bud in this way.

If you feel you can show this because the Plaintiff (a) has, by changing his address, shown that he might be able to evade you, or (b) is normally resident beyond the court's jurisdiction or (c) is suing for the benefit of another person or (d) has deliberately omitted or incorrectly stated his address in the writ, you may be able to obtain an order for security: Order 23, rule 1. (Although the court's original jurisdiction was inherent (as opposed to being derived from the rules), the categories have been confined to those above: 23/1-3/1.)

In the case of a **Plaintiff resident abroad**, the Master will principally be concerned with the Plaintiff's way of life and the presence or absence of assets within the jurisdiction: 23/1-3/3. If the Plaintiff, whether an individual or a company, can show, although permanently living abroad, that he has substantial property that is available and realisable to pay costs, you will not obtain an order; nor will security be ordered where the very subject matter of the action eg a painting or statue would cover the costs: 23/1-3/4.

Taking your own Legal Action

For the situation in the case of a limited company: see Section 726(1) of the Companies Act 1985 and 23/1-3/14, where liquidation would be tantamount to an inability to pay costs; though once again, the Master will be reluctant to cause the company to abandon a claim which has a fair prospect of success, by ordering any or excessive security to be given: 23/1-3/14.

You have to show that at the time of the application the company **would** not rather than **could** not pay the costs of the action: 23/1-3/14.

If your counterclaim is sufficiently bound up with your Defence, you will not be liable to an order against you, as this would effectively prevent you from defending but, if your counterclaim is in reality a totally separate action, you could, if living abroad, be ordered to give security: 23/1-3/8 and 23/1-3/16. Each case, however, will depend on its own particular facts: 23/1-3/8. It is possible for both you and the Plaintiff each to be ordered to give security: 23/1-3/8.

The Plaintiff will not have to give security simply because he is poor, insolvent, about to become bankrupt or already bankrupt and undischarged: 23/1-3/13; the case is different, however, on an appeal to the Court of Appeal: see 33 **APPEALS** and Order 59, rule 10(5). An ambassador but not his servant is immune from having to give security: 23/1-3/21. If you are sued by a Plaintiff, whose partner is against the action, the Plaintiff will have to give not only security to you but an indemnity to his partner and the action will be stayed until this has been done: 23/1-3/21. The fact that the Plaintiff is legally aided will not prevent him from having to give security: 23/1-3/23.

Initially write to the Plaintiff asking him to give security. If the Plaintiff's solicitor undertakes to secure your costs: 23/1-3/24, you need not apply. If he refuses, apply by summons with an affidavit in support in the usual way: 23/1-3/18. Although you should apply promptly, delay will not be decisive, unless you have allowed the Plaintiff to act to his detriment or he will suffer hardship in pursuing the action: 23/1-3/28.

Remember that, if, as the Defendant, you have commenced third party proceedings, you are in the position of a Plaintiff vis a vis the third party: 23/1-3/1.

When exercising his discretion, the Master will, without conducting a detailed consideration of the merits, take into account the likelihood of the Plaintiff winning, any admissions by you, any open offers or payments into court, delay in applying and, subject to your consent, any "without prejudice" negotiations: 23/1-3/2; if your own prospect of successfully defending is small, you will probably be refused security for costs. Similarly, say you admitted part of the Plaintiff's claim, you would effectively be able to obtain security yourself by making a payment into court and thus it will not be ordered: 23/1-3/2

The amount of security is always discretionary and unlikely to be equal to an estimate of the full costs: 23/1-3/29. Security is usually given by a payment into court: 23/1-3/26 but may be by a bond with two solvent sureties, who should not be the Plaintiff's solicitor: 23/1-3/27. If the Plaintiff fails to give the security ordered, his action will be dismissed: 23/1-3/30.

74 - EVIDENCE

See Section 30.

If the judge indicates that he is intending to give judgment in your favour by dismissing the Plaintiff's case without hearing your evidence, you still have the right to give evidence. This sounds strange but it could avoid complications, were the Plaintiff to appeal with the result that the Court of Appeal or House of Lords might have to remit the case for you to give evidence before they decide to reverse the judge's decision: 38/1/9.]

75 - INTERIM PAYMENTS

See Section 17 above. From your point of view as a Defendant, you may "show cause" either by (a) taking a technical point eg that, although it is a personal injuries case, you are uninsured or your means insufficient or by (b) showing on the merits that there is no certainty that the Plaintiff will succeed:Order 29, rule 11 and 29/11/1. Secondly, if you are one of two or more Defendants, it is not sufficient for the Plaintiff to show that he is bound to succeed against one of them. The Master must be satisfied that the Plaintiff will succeed against the particular party, in respect of whom an order to give security is made: 29/11/2.

76 - PAYMENTS INTO COURT

For an understanding of the concept and principles involved, see Section 21 above. Of specific interest to you, as Defendant, is that you should be careful (a) to take interest into account and (b) to make it clear where there is more than one cause of action, as to how much you have paid in in respect of each cause of action: Order 22, rule 1(4). You should either earmark separate payments in respect of each cause of action or state that your single payment covers all causes of action: 22/1/13 so as to avoid the Plaintiff applying for an order that you apportion the sum between or amongst the causes of action, which he may do if he is embarrassed by the effect of the payment into court: 22/1/3.

77 - DIRECTIONS

See Section 20. As it is generally the Plaintiff who issues the Summons for Directions, specific provision is made for you, as Defendant, to notify the Plaintiff, not less than seven days before the hearing of the summons, of any other orders or directions not sought by the Plaintiff, which you wish to be dealt with: Order 25, rule 7.

78 - APPEALS

See Section 33 *(c) Appeals to the Court of Appeal*, especially where it deals with **you as the Respondent**.

YOU THE DEFENDANT IN THE COUNTY COURT

79 - GENERAL

See Part 2 Sections 1-34, Part 3 Sections 35-62 and below.

80 - DEFENCE

It is well worth noting that by Section 49 of the County Courts Act 1984 the Plaintiff's bankrupcty provides a complete defence, **unless** the Plaintiff's Trustee in Bankruptcy elects to continue the action for the benefit of the Plaintiff's creditors and gives security for the costs of the action: CCR Order 5, rule 14.

If the Plaintiff's claim is for a particular sum, which you tendered for his acceptance before action and which he refused to accept, you have a defence of "tender before action" which you may plead in your Defence **provided** you pay the sum into court, when filing and delivering your Defence: CCR Order 9, rule 12. If you wish to allege that the summons or its service on you was irregular, you should still deliver your Defence: Order 9, rule13(1) but should not take any further step in the proceedings other than an application to strike them out within a reasonable time: Order 9, rule 13(2).

Should you wish to counterclaim against the Plaintiff **and some other person**, see CCR Order 9, rule 15, which incorporates RSC

Taking your own Legal Action

Order 15, rule 3 (not to be confused with **THIRD PARTY AND SIMILAR PROCEEDINGS**, which are dealt with by CCR Order 12 and RSC Order 16).

Should the Plaintiff **discontinue**, he should notify you and you may then generally claim your costs (by lodging a bill for taxation of your costs): Order 18, rule 2. Similarly, should you discontinue any counterclaim, the Plaintiff will be entitled to his costs: Order 18, rule 3.

81 - APPEALS

See Sections 33, 61 and 78 and in particular RSC Order 59, rule 3A, which requires you to certify the "value of the appeal" for an appeal to the Court of Appeal, and Order 59, rule 19 and the notes thereto, which deal with the procedure in detail.

82 - COSTS

See Sections 34 and 62 and also note 62/A4/38, which may well help you with regard to costs, where the Defendant sued you in the High Court but should have sued you in the County Court.

83 - IN THE SMALL CLAIMS COURT

See Sections 63, 64 and 65.

Form 1   525
Claim by the Driver of a Motor Van in Collision with a Motor Car at a Road Junction
1.   On   19   , the Plaintiff was driving his motor van along
, in the direction of   when the Defendant so negligently drove his Austin motor-car along   at its junction with
, that it collided with the Plaintiff's motor van.

Particulars of negligence

(a)   Driving too fast in the circumstances.
(b)   Failing to keep any or any proper look-out or to have any or any sufficient regard for other traffic that was or might reasonably be expected to be at the junction of these roads.
(c)   Emerging onto the   road without first ascertaining or ensuring that it was safe so to do.
(d)   Failing to give way to the Plaintiff while he was driving along the road.
(e)   Failing to give any or any adequate warning [or, signal] of his approach.
(f)   Failing to stop, to slow down, to swerve or in any other way so to manage or control his motorcar as to avoid the collision.

2.   By reason of these matters, the Plaintiff sustained injuries and has suffered loss and damage.

Particulars of injuries

[*Set these out in full detail*]

Particulars of special damage

[*Set out each item claimed separately*]
And the Plaintiff claims:

(i)   Damages;
(ii)   Interest on damages pursuant to section 35A of the Supreme Court Act 1981.

12

Form 2A - Claim by Principal against Agent for an Account of Debts Collected and Damages
1.   The Plaintiffs carry on a retail and credit business at   .
2.   By an agreement in writing dated   19   , the Plaintiffs agreed with the Defendants to employ the Defendant as their agent, to apply for and collect the debts due to the Plaintiffs from their customers and duly to account to the Plaintiffs therefor, and to pay him a commission of 5% on the amount so collected by him.
3.   There were implied terms of the said agreement, implied in order to give business efficacy thereto and/or by virtue of the relationship between the parties, an/or the Defendant owed to the Plaintiffs a duty of care to the effect that:

(i)   the Defendant would take all reasonable and proper steps and exercise all due diligence to collect the said debts;
(ii)   the Defendant would render a true and full account of all such debts collected by him;
(iii)   further or in the alternative the Defendant was under a fiduciary duty to the Plaintiff so to account;

4.   The Defendant has from time to time collected debts due to the Plaintiffs, but he has wrongfully and in breach of his contract and his said duties to the Plaintiff failed and refused to render a true or full account of all such debts collected by him. The Plaintiff is unable to give particulars until after discovery and/or the service of interrogatories.
5.   Further in breach of contract and duty, the Defendant failed to take all reasonable or proper steps to collect the said debts or to exercise all due diligence in that regard, such that the Plaintiff has lost payment of the said debts or part thereof and has suffered loss and damage.

Particulars of Breach of Contract and Duty

[*Set out the best particulars that can be given and add if necessary ... The above are the best particulars which the Plaintiff can give hereof until after discovery and/or the service of interrogatories*]

Particulars of Special Damage

[*State the nature and extent of the loss and damage claimed*]
6.   The Plaintiff is entitled to interest at such rate and for such periods as to the court may seem just pursuant to section 35A of the Supreme Court Act 1981.
And the Plaintiff claims:

(i)   An account of all debts collected by the Defendant from the Plaintiffs' customers and payment of the sum found due;
(ii)   Damages;
(iii)   Interest as aforesaid pursuant to section 35A of the Supreme Court Act 1981.

13

Form 2B - Claim by Principal against Agent for Breaches of Instructions
1.   By an oral agreement on or about   19   , the Plaintiff engaged the Defendant as an agent to purchase, if practicable, at   for the Plaintiff
tonnes of wheat of best quality, at a price not exceeding £   per quarter.
2.   It was an implied term of the said agreement, implied in order to give business efficacy to the same and/or by virtue of the relationship between the parties that the Defendant would comply with his instructions by the Plaintiff, further or in the alternative that he would use all reasonable endeavours and/or all due care and skill in so doing; further or in the alternative the Defendant owed to the Plaintiff a duty of care to the same effect.
3.   Negligently and/or in breach of contract the Defendant did not comply with the said instructions and/or although he could by reasonable diligence have purchased for the Plaintiff at   aforesaid   tonnes of wheat of best quality with the said limit of price:

(i)   the Defendant purchased for the Plaintiff only   tonnes of wheat;

143

| | (ii) | the wheat so purchased by him was of inferior quality in that ....[give particulars]. |

4.   By reason of the aforesaid, the Plaintiff has suffered loss and damage.

Particulars

[*Set out the nature and extent of the loss and damage claimed*]

5.   The Plaintiff further claims interest for such rate at such period as to the court may seem just pursuant to section 35A of the Supreme Court Act 1981.

And the Plaintiff claims:

| | (i) | Damages; |
| | (ii) | interest pursuant to section 35A of the Supreme Court Act 1981. |

Form 3 - Reply

| IN THE HIGH COURT OF JUSTICE | | 1997-S-No. |
| QUEENS BENCH DIVISION | | |

BETWEEN	SALT	**Plaintiff**
	and	
	PEPPER	**Defendant**

Reply

1.   The Plaintiff joins issue with the Defendant upon his Defence.

2.   If, for which the Plaintiff does not contend, Mr AB [was not the Defendant's agent/exceeded his authority as the Defendant's agent] as alleged in paragraph 3 of the Defence, the Plaintiff will say that the Defendant is estopped from denying that AB [was his agent/acted within the scope of his authority] because the Defendant held out AB as [his agent/having authority].

Particulars

The Plaintiff will rely, inter alia, on

| (a) | The Defendant's presence at the meeting held on 1 January 1997 between the Plaintiff and AB aforesaid; and |
| (b) | The Defendant's letter to the Plaintiff dated 10 January, a copy of which is annexed hereto, stated that the transaction should be concluded between the Plaintiff and AB. |

Served this   day of   1997.

[Plaintiff's name]
Plaintiff

Form 4 - Writ of Summons

| IN THE HIGH COURT OF JUSTICE | | 1995-P-No. 120 |
| QUEENS BENCH DIVISION | | |

BETWEEN	DAVID	**Plaintiff**
	and	
	JONATHAN	**Defendant**

[Formal parts of Writ of Summons form]

The Plaintiff's claim is for

(1)	Damages for breach of contract made by agreement dated 5 January 1996 between the Plaintiff and the Defendant;
(2)	Interest thereon pursuant to Section 35A of the Supreme Court Act 1981 as may be just;
(3)	A declaration that the Plaintiff's letter to the Defendant dated 24 December 1996 did not constitute notice of termination of the said agreement under Clause 16 thereof; and
(4)	An injunction restraining the Defendant by himself his servants or agents or otherwise howsoever from informing the Plaintiff's customers that the Plaintiff is no longer his agent for the sale of iguanas.

This Writ was issued by the said Plaintiff who resides at 1 The Lane, London N25 6AB.

Form 5A   No. PF 11

Summons under Order 14 for Whole Claim

[Title as in action]

Let all parties concerned attend the Master in Chambers in Room No.   , Central Office, Royal Courts of Justice, Strand, London WC2A 2LL, on   day the   day of   19   , at   o'clock in the   noon on the hearing of an application on the part of the Plaintiff for final judgment in this action against the Defendant [*or if against one or some of several Defendants, insert names*] for the amount claimed in the statement of claim with interest, if any, [*or as the case may be setting out the nature of the claim*] and costs.

Take notice that a party intending to oppose this application or to apply for a stay of execution should send to the opposite party, to reach him in sufficient time to enable him to reply and in any event not less than three days before the date above mentioned, a copy of any affidavit intended to be used.

Dated the   day of   19   .
This summons was taken out by the Plaintiff, of   .
To

Form 5B   No. PF 12

Summons under Order 14 for one or some of several claims

[Title as in action]

Let all parties concerned attend the Master in Chambers in Room No.   , Central Office, Royal Courts of Justice, Strand, London WC2A 2LL, on   day the   day of   19   , at   o'clock in the   noon on the hearing of an application by the Plaintiff for judgment in this action against the Defendant [*or if against one or some of several Defendants, insert names*] for the sum of £

[*or as the case may be*] being one [*or* some] of the claims, namely [*identifying or otherwise precisely specifying particular claim or claims referred to*] and the costs of this application.

Take notice that a party intending to oppose this application or to apply for a stay of execution should send to the opposite party, to reach him in sufficient time to enable him to reply and in any event not less than three days before the date above mentioned, a copy of any affidavit intended to be used.

Dated the   day of   19   .
This summons was taken out by the Plaintiff, of   .
To

Form 6   No. PF 10

Affidavit on Application under Order 14, rule 2, by or on behalf of Plaintiff

[Title as in action]

I,   of   [the above-named Plaintiff], make oath and say as follows:-

1.   The Defendant   is and was at the commencement of this action, justly and truly indebted to me, in the sum of £   . The particulars of the said claim appear by the statement of claim in this action.

2.   It is within my own knowledge that the said debt was incurred and is still due and owing as aforesaid
or
[2. I am informed by [*state source of information*] and I verily believe that the said debt was incurred and is still due and owing as aforesaid].

3.   I verily believe that there is no defence to this action [except as to the amount of damages claimed].

Sworn
This affidavit is filed on behalf of the Plaintiff

145

Form 7 - Reply and Defence to Counterclaim
IN THE HIGH COURT OF JUSTICE
QUEENS BENCH DIVISION
1996-L-No.

BETWEEN   LENNON   **Plaintiff**
                                             and
                                         MCCARTNEY   **Defendant**

Reply and Defence to Counterclaim

1.   The Plaintiff joins issue with the Defendant upon his Defence.
Defence to Counterclaim
2.   The Plaintiff says that the Defendant's claim for damages for personal injuries, arising from the accident on 31 December 1990,
        referred to in paragraph 10 of the Defence and Counterclaim, not having arisen within three years of this action, is barred by
        Section 11 of the Limitation Act 1980.

Served this   day of   1997.

                                                                              [Plaintiff's name]
                                                                                      Plaintiff

----

Form 8 - Supply of Further and Better Particulars

IN THE HIGH COURT OF JUSTICE   1996-F-No. 111
QUEENS BENCH DIVISION
Master
BETWEEN   FIRE   **Plaintiff**
                                             and
                                         BRIMSTONE   **Defendant**

**FURTHER AND BETTER PARTICULARS OF THE DEFENCE AND COUNTERCLAIM PURSUANT
TO THE [PLAINTIFF'S REQUEST/ORDER OF MASTER] DATED 8 DECEMBER 1996**

Under Paragraph 2
Of: "...in or about June 1995...the Plaintiffs showed the Defendant projected profits and thereby induced him to buy the said franchise..."
Request
21.   Naming the Plaintiff's agent alleged to have thus acted, identifying all relevant documents to be relied upon in support of this
        allegation and producing the same pursuant to CCR Order 14 rule 4.
Answer
John Smith in addition; the Defendant says that the Plaintiffs were in almost daily touch with and directing him in the day to day running of
the office and he further volunteers that:
(a)   The facts and matters relied on are apparent from the Plaintiffs' documents Items 6 and 7;
(b)   By his contract with the Plaintiffs (see Items 4 and 5), John Smith had express authority to sell franchises and therefore had
        implied authority to supply all information necessary to sell sub-franchises to prospective franchisees; and
(c)   The Plaintiffs knew that John Smith was selling franchises and were aware of the figures that were being used therefor.

Served this   day of January 1997

                                                                                   Defendant

----

Form 9 - List of documents for discovery
IN THE HIGH COURT OF JUSTICE   1997-V-No. 222
QUEENS BENCH DIVISION
BETWEEN   ANTONIO VIVALDI   **Plaintiff**
                                             and
                                      J   S   BACH   **First Defendant**
                                             and
                                      C   P   E   BACH   **Second Defendant**

LIST OF DOCUMENTS

The following is a list of the documents relating to the matters in question in this action which are or have been in the possession, custody or
power of the above-named Plaintiff and which is served in compliance with the Rules of the Supreme Court.
1.   The Plaintiff has in his possession, custody or power the documents relating to the matters in question in this action enumerated
in Schedule 1 hereto.
2.   The Plaintiff objects to produce the documents enumerated in Part 2 of the said Schedule 1 on the ground that they are, by their
very nature, privileged.
3.   The Plaintiff has had, but has not now in his possession, custody or power the documents relating to the matters in question in
this action enumerated in Schedule 2 hereto.

4.   Of the documents in Schedule 2 the same were last in the Plaintiff's possession, custody or power on the dates thereon.

5.   Neither the Plaintiff nor any other person on her behalf, have now, or ever had in their possession, custody or power any document of any description whatever relating to any matter in question in this action, other than the documents enumerated in Schedules 1 and 2 hereto.

SCHEDULE 1 - Part 1

ITEM	DESCRIPTION	DATE
1.	Copy Plaintiff's first manuscript for the Four Seasons	20 April 1715
2.	Letter Defendants to Plaintiff	13 January 1716
3.	Copy manuscript for Four Seasons with Defendant's notes	Various
4.	Copy receipt from Plagiarist Printers Ltd	10 October 1720

Part 2

Correspondence between Plaintiff and his solicitors.

SCHEDULE 2

The originals of those documents sent by the Plaintiff.

Dated the 25th day of October 1730.

NOTICE TO INSPECT

Take notice that the documents in the above list, other than those listed in Part 2 of Schedule 1 and Schedule 2 may be inspected at the offices of the Plaintiff, at The Conservatoire, Venice, during normal working hours on prior notice of three working days.

To the Defendants   Served the 25th day of October 1730
and their solicitors   by Antonio Vivaldi,
Johansen & Co,   The Conservatoire, Venice.
20 Right Street
London W20,   Plaintiff

Form 10 - Interrogatories
IN THE HIGH COURT OF JUSTICE   1997-G-No. 333
QUEENS BENCH DIVISION
BETWEEN: **MAXIM THREADBOLT**   Plaintiff
                                                and
                                         ANTIQUITY AUCTIONEERS   Defendants

----
INTERROGATORIES

On behalf of the above-named Plaintiff for the examination of the above-named Defendants.

1.   Did the Defendants furnish the Plaintiff with their standard Schedule?

2.   If the answer to the first interrogatory be in the affirmative, was the purpose thereof to obtain the Plaintiff's instructions so as to enable the Defendants to compose an entry in respect of the said Stradivarius in the catalogue for their auction sales?

3.   Look at the Plaintiff's description of the Stradivarius signed by the Plaintiff on 22 July 1953 (being Item 2 in the Plaintiff's list of documents). Did the Defendants receive this document?

4.   If the answer to the third interrogatory be in the affirmative, did the Defendants refer to the said document, when composing the catalogues for their auctions held on 4 October 1953 and 2 August 1955?

5.   If the answer to the third interrogatory be in the negative,
     (i)   What was the purpose for the Defendants having sent their Schedule to the Plaintiff?
     (ii) How and from what information did the Defendants compose the said entries in each of the said catalogues?

Take notice that the above interrogatories are to be answered by affidavit on or before 1 November 1956.

Delivered this 4th day of October 1956 by the Plaintiff.

To the above-named Defendants and their solicitors.

Form 11A   No. PF 65

Order (General Form) (O.32)

Mr. Justice   *[or Master*   *] in Chambers*

[Title as in action]

147

Upon hearing   and upon reading the affidavit of   sworn herein on the   day of   19   .
It is ordered that

1.
2.
3.
4.   The costs of this application be

Dated the   day of   19   .

Form 11B   No. 44

Judgment under Order 14 (O.14, r.3; O.42, r.1)

[Heading as in action]

Master [Mr. Justice]
The   day of   19   .
The Defendant having given notice of intention to defend herein and the Court having under Order 14, rule 3 ordered that judgment as hereinafter provided be entered for the Plaintiff against the Defendant,
it is this day adjudged that the Defendant do pay the Plaintiff £   and £   costs [*or* costs to be taxed].

or

Pay the Plaintiff damages to be assessed and costs [in the assessment] *or as may be according to the court's order.*

or

Deliver to the Plaintiff the goods described in the writ of summons [*or* statement of claim] as   [or pay the Plaintiff the value of the said goods to be assessed] [and also damages for their detention to be assessed] and costs [in the assessment] *or as may be according to the Court's order.*

Form 12 - Marking affidavit

    (i) [Plaintiff/Defendant]
    (ii) J. Smith [Name of maker]
    (iii) 1st [2nd/3rd - as the case may be]
    (iv) 3.1.97 [Date sworn]
    (v) "JS", "JS2" and "JS3" [indicating number of exhibits]

IN THE HIGH COURT OF JUSTICE   1997-G-No. 444
QUEENS BENCH DIVISION
Master Tiller
BETWEEN: **JADE GREEN**   **Plaintiff**
                                 and
                               ROSE PINK   **Defendant**

                               Affidavit

COURT STRUCTURE

TRIALS

HOUSE OF LORDS

COURT OF APPEAL
Appeal to House of Lords
under Section 1
Administration of Justice
(Appeals) Act 1934

HIGH COURT		COUNTY COURT		ARBITRATION
				(Small claims)
Judge (+ Jury)	**Master**	**District Judge**	**Judge** (+ Jury)	**Arbitrator**
Appeal under	(District Judge)	Appeal to Judge	Appeal to CA Setting Aside	
RSC Order 59,	Appeal to CA	under CCR Order 37,	under s77, County	of Award under
rule 3.	under RSC Order	rule 6.	Courts Act 1984 and	CCR Order 19,
	58, rule 2.		RSC Order 59, rule 19.	rule 8.

INTERLOCUTORY

HOUSE OF LORDS

COURT OF APPEAL
Appeal to House of Lords
under s1, Administration of
Justice (Appeals) Act 1934

HIGH COURT	COUNTY COURT	ARBITRATION
Judge in Chambers	**Judge**	**Judge**
Appeal to Court of Appeal	Appeal to Court of Appeal	Appeals to CA under S77
under RSC Order 58, rule 6.	under RSC Order 59, rule 19.	County Courts Act 1984
		and RSC Order 59, rule 19.
Master (District Judge)	**District Judge**	**Arbitrator**
Appeal to Judge in Chambers	Appeal to Judge under	Appeal to Judge
under RSC Order 58, rule 1.	CCR Order 13, rule 1.	as a rule of practice.

Tennakoons
SOLICITORS & COMMISSIONERS FOR OATHS
T. M. A. TENNAKOON, LL.B.